youthalpha.

LEADERS' GUIDE

Published in North America by Alpha North America, 2275 Half Day Road, Suite 185, Deerfield, IL 60015

© 2010 Alpha International, Holy Trinity Brompton, Brompton Road, London, SW7 1JA, UK

Youth Alpha Leaders' Guide

First printed by Alpha North America in 2010

Printed in the United States of America

Scripture in this publication is from the Holy Bible, New International Version (NIV), Copyright 1973, 1978, 1984 International Bible Society, used by permission of Zondervan. All rights reserved.

ISBN 978-1-934564-44-8

1 2 3 4 5 6 7 8 9 10 Printing/Year 14 13 12 11 10

ACKNOWLEDGEMENTS

The *Youth Alpha Leaders' Guide* is a truly global project. Alpha International would like to thank the many people from the international Youth Alpha team who have been involved in the creation and development of this resource, including:

Andy Watkins (Australia)
Beth Fellinger (Canada)
Chia Wen Chien (Singapore)
Dominik Sandles (Germany)
Francis Dodd (Ghana)
Jonathan Westerkamp (Netherlands)
Gisele Zurcher (Switzerland)
Helen Lawson (Scotland)
Ian Clarkson (England)
Jamie Haith (England)
Louisa Jacob (England)
Nicola Marshall (England)
Phil Knox (England)
Rachael Heffer (England)
Rebecca Long (USA)
Richard Dawson (England)
Richard Drake (New Zealand)
Sandra Blair (Scotland)
Scarlett Sharp (England)
Shane Linford (England)

This Youth Alpha material is based on *Alpha—Questions of Life* by Nicky Gumbel and has been compiled by Matt Costley. It is an updated and modified version of the 2003 edition, which was written by Jonathan Brant.

Special thanks to the following contributing authors: Mike Pilavachi, Mark Oestreicher, Pete Greig, Gavin Calver, Al Gordon, Greg Stier, Brad Hawkes, Simeon Whiting, Peter Carpentier, Greg and Essie Del Valle and also to Sophie Godfree, Philomena Lufkin and Julia Evans for all of their hard work on this project.

The Youth Alpha team would also like to thank the Alpha Publications team, including: Katie Markham, Kate Crossland-Page, Jo Soda, Will Ahern, Jon Shippen, Phil Williams, Becky Cotter, Lauren Eden, Mary Melo, Joe Laycock and Steven Wright.

youthalpha LEADERS' GUIDE

CONTENTS

SECTION 3 – YOUTH ALPHA TEAM TRAINING

APPENDICES

INTRODUCTION

WELCOME

"Don't let anyone look down on you because you are young, but set an example for the believers in speech, in life, in love, in faith and in purity" (1 Timothy 4:12).

Hi! We're thrilled that you've got a copy of this *Leaders' Guide* and that you are interested in running a Youth Alpha course.

This resource is designed to help you run a Youth Alpha course which, in turn, will help you to share your faith with your friends. We hope and pray that it enables you to do just that.

Youth Alpha is designed to be flexible because every group is different. Our hope is that this guide will help you to tailor a unique course perfectly suited to your group.

In every session, you will notice that each teaching point has several illustration options. Hopefully it will be clear to you which of these is best for your group. Please remember, however, that this resource is just a guide—feel free to add bits of your own story as you go and/or include your own ideas for illustrating the points.

We would also encourage you to access the Youth Alpha TalkBuilder online at youthalpha.org.

TalkBuilder is an exciting new tool that will allow you to:
- build and personalize your Youth Alpha talks online

- find more illustration options

- upload any illustrations that you have used to share with others

Before you get into the main part of the resource, we want to give you a few practical tips that will help you to run a successful Youth Alpha course:

1 Run the whole course – don't cut sessions out
Our experience is that this is the best way to run Youth Alpha—if it wasn't, we wouldn't have put all the sessions in! You will notice that there are two "combined" talks, in which the topics of four sessions have been squeezed into two. This merging will allow you to cover all the course material over eight weeks, rather than ten, if you need to.

2 Do the Youth Alpha Weekend or Day
We know that the course Weekend or Day can be difficult to organize; it does require a lot of effort, but it is one of the most important parts of the course.

3 Register your course online
Go to alphausa.org/youth and sign up. This will mean potential guests wanting to do a course in your area can find you.

4 Get in touch with your local Youth Alpha Advisor
Youth Alpha Advisors are amazing people with a wealth of experience in running Youth Alpha. If you have any questions, or if you need a bit of help, contacting your local Youth Alpha Advisor is a great place to start. Go to alphausa.org/youthadvisors to find out who your local Advisor is.

5 Come to a Youth Alpha Conference or training day
This guide includes everything you need to know to run a great course, but it's even better if you can come and get some training: check out alphausa.org/youth for more information. We hope to see you at a training event soon!

The last thing we want to say is: please get in touch—we would love to hear from you! We especially enjoy hearing stories of lives being changed through Youth Alpha, so whatever it is, drop us a line at youthalpha@alphausa.org anytime.

We are praying for you, and we hope you have a fantastic time running Youth Alpha.

The Youth Alpha team

WHAT IS YOUTH ALPHA?

Youth Alpha is an adaptation of the Alpha course. The Alpha course gives people an opportunity to explore the meaning of life and the Christian faith.

A BRIEF HISTORY

The Alpha course has been running at Holy Trinity Brompton (HTB—a church in central London) since the late 1970s, when it was started as a course for new Christians. In the early 1990s, a clergyman called Nicky Gumbel (now Sr. Pastor of HTB) took over the leadership of Alpha and soon noticed the potential to use it as an evangelistic tool.

After seeing so many people come to faith on the course at HTB, other churches in London also began running Alpha. It soon started to spread throughout the UK, and then all around the world. It is now running in over 160 countries, and it is estimated that over 15 million people have attended an Alpha course.

A typical Alpha session starts with some food, which is followed by a "talk" explaining a particular aspect of the Christian faith. This is followed by a discussion in small groups. Generally, the small group time is considered the most important part of the course, as it is a chance for guests to say whatever they like; they are encouraged to discuss the talk honestly.

YOUTH ALPHA

Youth Alpha is very similar to "classic" Alpha in terms of teaching content, but it is presented in a way that is more appealing to young people.

Youth Alpha was started in 1996 as a response to the demand from churches for a youth version of the Alpha course. It was redeveloped in 2002, and this version was launched in 2010.

Youth Alpha is now running all across the globe, from Uganda to the United States, from Singapore to Spain, and from Argentina to Australia.

The course is being used in all major denominations and in many different contexts: in schools, confirmation classes, young offenders institutions, youth groups, youth clubs, sports clubs, and coffee shops. Time and again we have been excited to see the number of young people starting to run the course in order to share their faith with their friends.

The first Youth Alpha Conference was held in 2004. Since then, many more have been held worldwide, and many thousands of delegates have attended these events.

The Youth Alpha course covers the following topics:

Introductory session – Christianity: Boring, Untrue, and Irrelevant?
Session 1 – Who Is Jesus?
Session 2 – Why Did Jesus Die?
Session 3 – How Can We Have Faith?
Session 4 – Why and How Do I Pray?
Session 5 – Why and How Should I Read the Bible?
Session 6 – How Does God Guide Us?

Youth Alpha Weekend/Day

Weekend Session 1 – What about the Holy Spirit?
Weekend Session 2 – How Can I Be Filled with the Holy Spirit?
Weekend Session 3 – How Can I Make the Most of the Rest of My Life?

Session 7 – How Can I Resist Evil?
Session 8 – Why and How Should I Tell Others?
Session 9 – Does God Heal Today?
Session 10 – What about the Church?

So, by running Youth Alpha, you are joining many others across the globe in using this tool to help share the good news of Jesus Christ. It's great to have you on board.

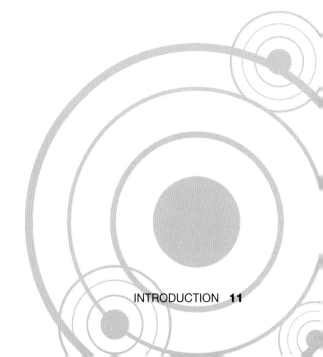

A TYPICAL YOUTH ALPHA SESSION

In one sense, there's no such a thing as a "typical" Youth Alpha session, since every course will be different, but there are four key elements that should form the basis of every course, regardless of style and context: food, fun, the talk, and small groups.

FOOD

One of the reasons that the regular Alpha course has worked so well is that at every session the guests eat together. We think there's something quite spiritual about people eating together. It is a way of helping people to feel comfortable and at ease, and it forms community. Eating together was definitely of high value for Jesus too—just look at the Gospels to see how much of Jesus' ministry was based around shared meals.

So we want to encourage you to fit the principle of eating together into the context of your Youth Alpha course. No doubt this will be very different from course to course. Think about what sort of food your friends are into, and where teenagers in your area eat together. Probably only you will know what is best.

It might be that you get takeout pizzas, or recruit some parents to cook a great meal. Other courses have gone for the coffee shop feel with muffins and pastries, while some have bought hot dogs for everyone. In a school lunchtime, food is harder to do, so perhaps you might offer cookies to go with everyone's packed lunch. Our recommendation is that you make food a key part of the course, but how you do that is up to you.

NB: it's worth remembering that guests on the course aren't usually Christians and we need to make them feel as comfortable as possible. Therefore, we never pray before eating on Youth Alpha. This prevents people from feeling uncomfortable. There will be opportunities to pray later on the in course.

FUN

We believe that it is possible to learn about Jesus and have fun doing it (radical, aren't we?), so we would encourage you to make your course as fun as possible.

When you're inviting people to Youth Alpha, don't ask them to sign up for the whole course, just ask them to come to the first week. If they like it, they will come back. We have found this works best for two reasons: first, the idea of joining an eight (nine or ten) week course can seem pretty intense; secondly, if we know that people will only come back next time if this session is fantastic, we will put more effort into making the first week fun. We recommend spending an extra twenty minutes or so making the venue look good, as this can really add to the fun feel of the course.

In this guide, each Youth Alpha session starts with a choice of ice breaker games. These are silly games, designed to get everyone involved and having fun. If you don't like them or don't feel they will suit your group, then don't use them—use your own ideas instead (don't forget to share these with us online at alphausa.org/youth!).

TALK/PRESENTATION

Obviously, what we're doing on Youth Alpha is a factual exercise: we are passing on knowledge —Biblical truth—and encouraging people to explore this and think it through for themselves.

Over ten weeks (or eight or nine, depending on your course), everyone who does Youth Alpha is given a crash course in Christianity along with the basic building blocks of faith. We're passing on factual knowledge, but we do it in a more creative way than just talking at our guests.

There is no DVD for Youth Alpha. Unlike most regular Alpha sessions, which use DVDs of Nicky Gumbel, the Youth Alpha talks are always given live. This may be a scary thought for some of you (enough to make you think twice about running a course!) but it is definitely the best way. And you can do it!

The good news is that each of the talks is clearly laid out for you in this guide, as well as on TalkBuilder. There are lots of different options to choose from (movie clips, internet video clips, stories, games, and activities) to help illustrate what you are saying. A Youth Alpha talk should be between ten and twenty minutes in length.

For further information on how to give a great Youth Alpha talk, please see page 45.

SMALL GROUPS

Following the talk (or as part of it) we always have small groups.

A typical small group consists of between six and eight guests, one or two leaders who facilitate the discussion, and one or two "helpers" who are there to host and welcome people.

Small groups are arguably the most important part of the Youth Alpha course. The reasons are twofold:

1 Small groups can be the part of the course that really engages people; it is where the relational side of the course kicks in and where friendships develop. We all know how important it is to feel like we're part of a group.

2 It is where we give space for the group to say what they feel and allow God's Spirit to work. We genuinely value the opinion of everyone on the course, regardless of how "wacky" that may be. There's no better way to encourage learning and discovery than through discussion.

There is an article in Section 2 of this guide called "How to lead a Youth Alpha small group" (see page 42) which is absolutely essential reading for anyone running Youth Alpha. There is also a "team training" talk outline called "How to lead small groups on Youth Alpha" in Section 3 of this guide (see page 75).

IS YOUTH ALPHA FOR YOU?

This may not be the first question you'd expect to be asked at the start of this resource, but it could be one of the most important ones.

Youth Alpha may not be the best course for you. We encourage you to think and pray through whether to start using this tool. Do you have the resources, and support to make it happen?

If you want to share your faith with a group of people with whom you are already on a journey or doing life with, then Youth Alpha might be a great thing to do together.

Some questions to ask yourself before you commit:

• Why do I/we want to run a Youth Alpha course?	GOOD IDEA ☐	GOD IDEA ☐
• Is this about converting people, or sharing my faith out of love?	CONVERTING ☐	SHARING ☐
• Do I/we have the time and resources to be able to do this?	NO ☐	YES ☐
• What next? What if all of my group become Christians? What about those who enjoy the course but don't become Christians?	NO IDEA ☐	GOT A PLAN ☐
• Do I/we have the support of my church, parents, friends, etc.?	NO ☐	YES ☐
• Are there some people praying for me/us?	NO ☐	YES ☐
• Is my church willing to welcome any of our group who may want to join?	NO ☐	YES ☐

If you checked any of the first column, then it might be worth giving a bit more thought to whether the timing is right for you to run a course. If you checked all of the right-hand column, then you're ready to start planning your Youth Alpha course!

HOW TO USE THIS LEADERS' GUIDE

Whether you are fifteen or fifty-one (actually, especially if you are fifteen!), this resource has been written for you. One of the exciting things that God seems to have been doing with Youth Alpha over the last few years is inspiring teenagers to run the course for their friends.

We really want to encourage that, so if you are a teenager, know that we believe in you and want to support you. If you are a bit older, then we want to support you too—but why not involve some of your youth group in the planning and leadership of the course? Our experience shows us that this is the best way.

This *Youth Alpha Leaders' Guide* is full of helpful information and has been designed to give someone with no experience in leading this kind of course enough confidence to give it a go. On the other hand, you may well be a youth ministry veteran and a lot of this may seem very basic. We would encourage you to flick through all of the material and take in whatever is relevant to you.

The *Leaders' Guide* contains four main sections along with appendices:

SECTION 1 – HOW TO RUN A GREAT YOUTH ALPHA COURSE

This section tells you everything you need to know in order to run a great course. It includes helpful checklists to make sure all the details of your course are accounted for.

SECTION 2 – EXPERT ADVICE ON RUNNING YOUTH ALPHA

This section contains articles on the many different aspects of running a Youth Alpha course, all of which are written by youth ministry professionals.

SECTION 3 – YOUTH ALPHA TEAM TRAINING

This section contains full talk outlines for the two team training sessions. This will help you to equip your team to run the course successfully.

APPENDICES

This section contains all the appendices that are referred to throughout this *Leaders' Guide*. Each appendix contains additional information that will help you to run your course.

We hope that you will find this *Leaders' Guide* helpful. Enjoy!

SECTION 1

HOW TO RUN A GREAT YOUTH ALPHA COURSE

PLANNING YOUR YOUTH ALPHA COURSE

So you've decided that you'd like to run a Youth Alpha course? That's great! The next thing to do is start figuring out some practical details.

A successful Youth Alpha course will require a fair bit of planning, but don't worry—it's easier than you think. Most of us probably think we can organize a course in less time than it takes in reality, so the sooner you start thinking about it the better.

The more work you do in advance and the better prepared you and your team are, the the more relaxed you'll be on the course itself. This will free you up to spend more time building friendships with people and making them feel valued.

PLANNING – STAGE 1 (3–6 months in advance)

THINGS TO CONSIDER

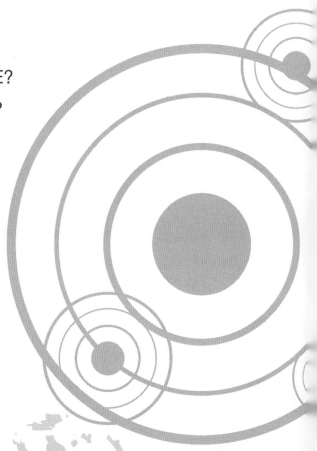

1. DO I HAVE THE SUPPORT OF MY PASTOR/YOUTH PASTOR/ CHURCH LEADER?

2. WHAT IS THE AIM OF THE COURSE?

3. WHO IS THE COURSE FOR?

4. WHERE WILL THE COURSE TAKE PLACE?

5. WHEN WILL THE COURSE TAKE PLACE?

6. WHO WILL RUN IT?

7. HOW DO WE PAY FOR IT?

8. WHAT ABOUT THE WEEKEND/DAY?

9. SHOULD WE HAVE SUNG WORSHIP?

10. WHO IS MY YOUTH ALPHA ADVISOR?

11. HAVE I REGISTERED MY COURSE?

1 DO I HAVE THE SUPPORT OF MY PASTOR/YOUTH PASTOR/ CHURCH LEADER?

We would strongly encourage you to get the support of your church before you set out to run a Youth Alpha course. If you are part of a youth group, this might mean chatting to your youth pastor to get their support. It doesn't necessarily mean you are asking for their help, but you do want their blessing. Ideally, you will need their support in prayer, goodwill, and possibly with money.

If you are a youth leader, sit down with your church leader, explain the vision to them and ask for their support.

"How good and pleasant it is when brothers and sisters live together in unity!" (Psalm 133:1).

2 WHAT IS THE AIM OF THE COURSE?

To some, this might seem like a pretty obvious question. While Youth Alpha is an evangelistic course, there are also other ways to use it. Some reasons for running Youth Alpha include using it:

- As a course for those who are outside the church—for evangelism
- As a tool for discipleship
- For renewing and deepening previous faith commitments
- As part of a course to lead up to baptism or confirmation (some denominations)—see page 57

It is important that you decide from the outset what the aim of your course is. Experience shows that if you try to use the course for more than one of these reasons you will probably not be so successful.

3 WHO IS THE COURSE FOR?

Again, this may seem like a pretty obvious question, but it is definitely worth thinking about. Who will you invite on your course?

Possibilities include:

- Your friends
- Those who live in your local community
- Those already involved in your church (if you are using Youth Alpha as a discipleship tool)
- Those who have had some contact with church, but haven't really been involved
- Those in a local club or organization (eg: YFC center or youth club)
- Those in a local school (e.g.: lunchtime or after school club)

4 WHERE WILL THE COURSE TAKE PLACE?

This is an important thing to think about. The venue you choose could be the difference between people feeling comfortable or not, and consequently, people coming or not. We want to remove any potential obstacles that may get in the way of someone coming to Jesus. Here are some ideas and things to think about.

How many people might come? It's worth considering this, as the last thing you want is to have a room big enough for forty people if only five turn up. It is far better to use a small room and squeeze people in. Be realistic about how many people might come.

Potential venues include:

Churches – for many people running the course, this is the first option that springs to mind. However, just because there is space available at your church, and just because it's probably free, doesn't mean it is the best idea. While it's probably okay if you are running a course for people with a link to the church, for others, going into a church might be an extra hurdle to overcome.

Community centers – generally these are intended to serve the community and, therefore, are not too expensive to rent.

> *"How good and pleasant it is when brothers and sisters live together in unity!" (Psalm 133:1)*

Sports centers – well worth considering for courses with younger teenagers who will relish the opportunity to play some energetic games. It is also worth considering for courses with guests who are seriously into sports.

Schools – if you are running a lunchtime or after-school course, then asking your school for a classroom to use is probably the best option (for more information on this, please see the article on page 58).

Your/someone's home – if you are aiming to run a small-sized course, then this may well be the best option. Going to either your home, or the home of one of your friends might be more chilled out than an "official" building.

Fast food restaurants – if the people you want to invite spend lots of time at places like McDonalds, then this is another option. Many restaurants have small side rooms (often used for kids' parties, etc.) that they might be willing to let you use/rent (you will probably have to promise to consume a specified quantity of burgers and soft drinks!).

Coffee shop – similarly, if this sort of dynamic fits your group it may work. We've heard lots of stories about large coffee shop chains being willing to let groups rent their coffee shop after hours if they commit to buying a minimum number of drinks, etc.

Youth clubs etc. – if there is a youth club or youth center in your community you might be able to use this for a minimal fee.

You may well have a much better idea that is different to any of the above—if so, go for it! Don't forget to let us know where you ran a course and how it went for you—email youth@alpha.org

5 WHEN WILL THE COURSE TAKE PLACE?

Before settling on a day or a time, you will need to do think about who you are inviting to your course and what their lives are like. For example, you don't want to pick a time and day that clashes with football practice, etc. The first rule of making this kind of decision is to realize that you may never find a time that is perfect for everybody, but try to exclude as few people as possible by considering these questions:

- What time does school finish?
- How easy is it to get to the venue—will guests need a ride or can they get there by themselves?
- What kind of evening/weekend commitments do they already have (clubs, jobs, sports teams, night to go out on the town, homework, family, etc.)?
- How do their parents feel about them going out on week nights?
- When are school exams?

We would also recommend fitting the course into a school semester. Our experience is that if school vacations fall in the middle of the course, it is very difficult to restart and get people back into the course after a few weeks off (if a vacation falls during your course, you may wish to stop for a week if people are going away). It is far better to start at the beginning of the semester and fit the whole course in to eight or ten weeks. We suggest that you avoid running the course at the same time as final exams.

Ideally, the Youth Alpha Weekend/Day should come after Session 5 and before Session 8 (see course outlines). Don't forget to schedule the two team training events: Session 1 before the course starts, and Session 2 just before the weekend or day away. For sample schedules for your Youth Alpha course, please see Appendix 1 on page 104, or online at alphausa.org/youthdownloads.

OPTION 1 – TEN WEEK COURSE (PLUS LAUNCH EVENT)

Team training session 1 – How to lead small groups on Youth Alpha

Introductory session – Christianity: Boring, Untrue, and Irrelevant?
Session 1 – Who Is Jesus?
Session 2 – Why Did Jesus Die?
Session 3 – How Can We Have Faith?
Session 4 – Why and How Do I Pray?
Session 5 – Why and How Should I Read the Bible?
Session 6 – How Does God Guide us?

Team training session 2 – How to pray for each other on Youth Alpha

Youth Alpha Weekend/Day

Weekend Session 1 – What about the Holy Spirit?
Weekend Session 2 – How Can I Be Filled with the Holy Spirit?
Weekend Session 3 – How Can I Make the Most of the Rest of My Life?

Session 7 – How Can I Resist Evil?
Session 8 – Why and How Should I Tell Others?
Session 9 – Does God Heal Today?
Session 10 – What about the Church?

OPTION 2 – NINE WEEK COURSE (PLUS LAUNCH EVENT)

Team training session 1 – How to lead small groups on Youth Alpha

Introductory session – Christianity: Boring, Untrue, and Irrelevant?
Session 1 – Who Is Jesus?
Session 2 – Why Did Jesus Die?
Session 3 – How Can We Have Faith?
Session 4 – Why and How Do I Pray?
Session 5 – Why and How Should I Read the Bible?
Session 6 – How Does God Guide us?

Team training session 2 – How to pray for each other on Youth Alpha

Youth Alpha Weekend/Day

Weekend Session 1 – What about the Holy Spirit?
Weekend Session 2 – How Can I Be Filled with the Holy Spirit?
Weekend Session 3 – How Can I Make the Most of the Rest of My Life?

Session 7 – How Can I Live Free? *["How Can I Resist Evil?" and
            "Does God Heal Today?" combined]*
Session 8 – Why and How Should I Tell Others?
Session 9 – What about the Church?

OPTION 3 – EIGHT WEEK COURSE (PLUS LAUNCH EVENT)

Team training session 1 – How to lead small groups on Youth Alpha

Introductory session – Christianity: Boring, Untrue, and Irrelevant?
Session 1 – Who Is Jesus?
Session 2 – Why Did Jesus Die?
Session 3 – How Can We Have Faith?
Session 4 – Why and How Do I Pray?
Session 5 – Why and How Should I Read the Bible?
Session 6 – How Does God Guide us?

Team training session 2 – How to pray for each other on Youth Alpha

Youth Alpha Weekend/Day

Weekend Session 1 – What about the Holy Spirit?
Weekend Session 2 – How Can I Be Filled with the Holy Spirit?
Weekend Session 3 – How Can I Make the Most of the Rest of My Life?
Session 7 – How Can I Live Free? *["How Can I Resist Evil?" and "Does God Heal Today?" combined]*
Session 8 – What about the Church and Telling Others? *["Why and How Should I Tell Others?" and "What about the Church?" combined]*

---

6 WHO WILL RUN IT?

So far, there's just you. Who else can help you? What kind of team are you going to need? The more people you can involve in your team, the more people there are praying for the course and inviting people.

Talks – who will do the talks? Don't just automatically think of asking your youth leaders! We would encourage you to do the talks yourself. The sessions in this guide have been written to make it as easy as possible for anyone to give a talk, even if they have never done so before.

Small group leaders – who will be the small group leaders? If you've run the course before, why not ask some of the people who came on the last course as guests to help lead groups?

Food – are you going to need people to help you get or make food?

Set up/take down – what about people to help set up and take down?

It might be the case that there are people in your church who wouldn't see themselves as natural youth leaders, but would still love to support you. They may be willing to help set up, take down, or help you with the provision of food. You could enlist the help of some parents to take turns helping bring food.

Note to youth pastors: we would really encourage you to get as many young people as you can on your team. There is no doubt in our minds that the best people to share their faith with teenagers are teenagers! Traditionally, the church has been slow to learn that, but things seem to be changing. We encourage you to see your role as helping to equip teenagers to reach their friends; Youth Alpha gives you a brilliant opportunity to do that. You may find it is one of the best means of discipleship you've ever found!

7 HOW DO WE PAY FOR IT?

We really believe that running a Youth Alpha course doesn't need to cost the earth. Many of the illustrations require very little in terms of material, though there are some items that you will need to buy.

One important principle that Alpha has always run on is that the course should be free for guests. We usually suggest that asking people to make a small donation for the food is fine, as is charging for the cost of the Weekend/Day, but ideally, no one should be prevented from attending any part of the course because of money.

It is worth chatting to someone who is good with budgets and making a list of what the course might cost (including the Weekend/Day—venue hire, transportation, etc). When you have an idea of the sum of money needed, you could chat to your pastor/church leader or other contacts to see if they can help, or you can do some fundraising yourself. Some churches have a youth or missions' budget that they may be thrilled to use to support what you are doing. You are far more likely to receive some financial support if you explain your needs and apply well in advance.

8 WHAT ABOUT THE WEEKEND/DAY AWAY?
The Youth Alpha Weekend/Day is a key part of the course—there is more information on how to plan it later in this section.

9 SHOULD WE HAVE SUNG WORSHIP?
On an adult Alpha course, worship is considered a viable part of the program if the course has more than thirty people. We believe that this is the critical mass required for singing songs without embarrassment.

Obviously, the dynamics of a Youth Alpha course are different. Only you will know if worship would be appropriate for your course, and, if it *is* appropriate, what kind of worship would be most natural for your group. It will depend on who is coming on the course, the size of your team, and whether you have a gifted worship leader available to you.

More information on this can be found in "Worship on Youth Alpha" (see page 55).

10 WHO IS MY YOUTH ALPHA ADVISOR?
Thousands of Youth Alpha courses have already taken place across the globe. In many countries there are Youth Alpha Advisors (visit the Alpha website, alphausa.org/youthadvisors to see who is local to you) who can give you invaluable help and advice. As well as giving you advice from their own experience, they may also be able to put you in contact with someone nearby who is already running a successful course, or direct you to a Youth Alpha conference. Chances are that a short chat with an Advisor will save you loads of time and effort in the long run.

11 HAVE I REGISTERED MY COURSE?
We would strongly encourage you to visit alphausa.org/youth and register your course online. This means that people who are visiting the site looking for a course to join can find you more easily. You'll be the first to hear of new Youth Alpha developments and you'll also get regular updates from the Youth Alpha team.

PLANNING – STAGE 2 (1–2 months in advance)

THINGS TO CONSIDER

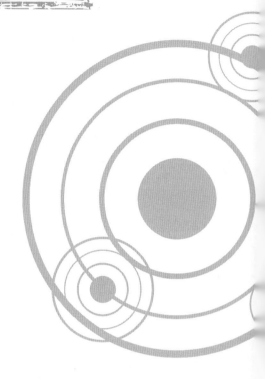

1. HOW DO I ADVERTISE MY COURSE?
2. WHAT EQUIPMENT WILL I NEED?
3. WHO IS THE COURSE FOR?
4. WHAT ABOUT A LAUNCH EVENT?
5. HOW DO SMALL GROUPS WORK?
6. WHO SHOULD LEAD THE SMALL GROUPS?
7. DO WE PRAY IN THE SMALL GROUPS?
8. HOW DO I TRAIN MY TEAM?
9. WHAT ABOUT THE PRACTICAL ISSUES?

1 HOW DO I ADVERTISE MY COURSE?

Most, if not all, of the people who attend your course will come because of a personal invitation. While a brochure, poster, or invitation on its own is unlikely to bring someone to the course, well-produced advertising can help increase confidence and make it much easier for people to take a risk and invite their friends. In most cases, you and your team will need to invite people personally.

Youth Alpha have produced posters and postcards which can be used to advertise the course. You can get creative and use the Internet (sites such as *Facebook* are great) to advertise the course, or you could make a short film advertisement to circulate.

There is a sample information sheet, explaining what the course is about, that can be given to the parents of those you are inviting (see Appendix 2 on page 105. For sample Parent Cards, please visit alphausa. org/youthdownloads).

2 WHAT EQUIPMENT WILL I NEED?

Read through the sessions and, based on which illustrational options you choose, figure out what you will need to run the course. For example, you may need a computer, a DVD player, a TV, or a projector. Can you borrow any of these items from a church or a friend? Which DVDs will you need over the weeks—can you borrow these from friends? Be organized about planning for this so you don't get caught at the last minute (see page 53 for more information on how to use multimedia).

3 WHO IS PRAYING FOR THE COURSE?

Is there a group of people you know (perhaps from your church) who might commit to praying for you and your course? Could you ask them?

4 WHAT ABOUT A LAUNCH EVENT?

See page 28 for more information on how to plan and run a Launch Event.

5 HOW DO SMALL GROUPS WORK?

Small groups are a key part of the course. There are two ways to do small groups on Youth Alpha—either in small bursts in between the teaching points, or at the end of the talk. The suggested questions at the end of each session are designed to work either way. You will know which option will work best for your group.

Small groups usually have between eight and twelve members, but there should never be more than twelve people in a group. Ideally, each group should have one or two "leaders" and one or two "helpers," plus between six and eight "guests"— people who are there to do the course but aren't on the team.

The leader(s) are there to guide the discussion and host the group. Normally, leaders are Christians who have done the course before. The helpers are there to help host the group and to make guests feel welcome. They may help get drinks and food for people, make introductions and generally be encouraging and helpful, but they shouldn't talk in the discussion.

Allocating people to small groups requires great skill. Depending on the age and maturity of your group, you may wish to form single sex groups, or mix it up (our experience is that younger youth do better in single sex groups and mid/older teenagers do better in mixed groups). We have found that groups work best when teenagers of similar ages are put together. You must also be conscious of the fact that those who have brought friends along may like to be in the same group as their guests. If you know who is coming, it is helpful to allocate people to groups before the course starts, but be prepared to be flexible at the first session.

We would strongly encourage you to do the team training sessions with your team, as the first of these focuses on how small groups work (see Section 3, page 73 for more information).

If you have more than one small group, think about where each group will meet for their discussion time. Wherever they are, everyone in the group must feel comfortable and safe. A useful tip is to ensure that everyone sits on the same level—either on chairs, sofas, or the floor, but not a combination of these, as it will make the group dynamic feel odd.

It is vital that all small groups finish on time, if not early. It is better to leave people wanting more than letting them get bored—you can always continue the discussion next time. Be ruthless about sticking to your finish time—even if someone is making the best point ever!

For more information on small groups see "How to lead a Youth Alpha small group" on page 42.

6 WHO SHOULD LEAD THE SMALL GROUPS?

Having good small group leaders is key to the success of your Youth Alpha course. These are the people who will be hosting the groups and who will have the most contact with the guests who come.

A good way to decide if someone is right to facilitate a small group discussion is to ask yourself the question, "Would I want my best non-Christian friend to be in this person's small group?" If the answer is "no" then they may not be the best person to have as a small group leader.

Commitment

It is important to make sure that your team are aware of the commitment required to help on Youth Alpha before they agree to take part. Be brave and tell the team up front that they are expected to commit to:

- The launch event

- The whole course (obviously)

- The team training sessions

- The Weekend/Day

- Praying for each member of their group every day

It's a bit like being a part of a sports team or a drama production—if you sign up for it, you need to be able to commit or it won't work. Of course, this only applies to the team, not to the guests.

7 DO WE PRAY IN THE SMALL GROUPS?

One of the goals of the small group is to model praying together, but it is important to remember not to rush into it. There may be people in the group for whom Youth Alpha is their first experience of anything church-related; they may not be comfortable praying with everyone else until later in the course. Go at the pace of the slowest person in your group—if they aren't ready, don't do it.

The earliest we would suggest you try praying together is in Session 4, after the talk "Why and how do I pray?" If you do decide to have a time of prayer, the leader should test the waters by suggesting that it might be cool if the group prayed together.

Make it clear that no one has to pray aloud, but they're all welcome to. We suggest that the small group leader prays a very short and simple prayer first, something like, "Thank you, God, for the weather. Amen." If the leader prays the world's most powerful and beautiful prayer, chances are the group will think, "Wow, if that's what prayer is, I could never do that." If we pray a simple prayer, however, the group may think, "Hey, that was simple. I could do way better than that," and they probably will!

8 HOW DO I TRAIN MY TEAM?

We suggest running two Team Training events —the first, "How to lead small groups on Youth Alpha" should be held before the course begins, and the second, "How to pray for each other on Youth Alpha" should be held before the Youth Alpha Weekend or Day.

Training your team is important, even if your group leaders have led small groups before. The training events provide an important opportunity for your team to get together and pray for the course.

Talk outlines for these two training sessions are included in Section 3 of this resource, please see pages 75 and 91 for more information.

9 WHAT ABOUT THE PRACTICAL ISSUES?

At this point, it is worth making a plan detailing how the course will run. This will make things simple rather than stressful! Think about:

- Who will help set up the venue each week?

- Who will sort out DVD clips, online videos/ resources and other media? (for more information on this, please see page 53)

- Who will help with food and drinks each week?

- Who will help clean up after each session?

PLANNING YOUR YOUTH ALPHA LAUNCH EVENT

Often, it is a great idea to have some sort of "launch event" to help advertise your course. The idea behind this is to host a relaxed and fun event to which people can bring their friends—in particular, their friends who aren't already part of the church—so they can hear a bit about Youth Alpha, and hopefully enjoy it enough to join your course.

A launch event can be a good way to give people who may initially be put off by the thought of doing a "course" a chance to experience Youth Alpha without having to commit. The same applies to those who have never been to a Christian event before.

The general format for a launch event is to focus on the social, fun aspect of Youth Alpha, and, to have a short presentation on the upcoming Youth Alpha course. The presentation should include the testimonies of several people (or just one, if time is tight) and the first talk in the session material entitled, "Christianity: Boring, Untrue, and Irrelevant?"

Obviously, you will want to keep the presentation fairly brief while making it as interesting and thought-provoking as possible. At the end of the presentation or at the end of the event, fliers for, or invitations to the upcoming Youth Alpha course should be handed out, and an opportunity should be given for people to sign up for the course on the spot.

PLANNING – (1–2 months in advance)

THINGS TO CONSIDER

1. WHAT TYPE OF EVENT WILL WE RUN?
2. WHO IS GOING TO HELP US?
3. WHERE WILL WE HOLD OUR LAUNCH EVENT?
4. WHAT SORT OF ENTERTAINMENT DO WE WANT?
5. HOW WILL WE ADVERTISE OUR EVENT?
6. HOW MUCH WILL IT COST?

1 WHAT TYPE OF EVENT WILL WE RUN?

Feel free to create your own type of Launch Event, but to get you started, here are some suggestions. You could organize:

- A performance by a local band, or even a "battle of the bands" with a number of local youth bands

- A sports competition, e.g.: five-a-side football, table tennis, basketball, skating, whatever you think would appeal to your group

- A club night with music, videos, and drinks (non-alcoholic!)

- A mini-Olympics or an "it's a knockout competition" with loads of messy games

- A themed banquet

- A '70s or '80s disco

- A film night, with a recent blockbuster projected onto the biggest screen you can muster up (some groups have hired a cinema for this)

Only you know what budget and facilities you have available, and only you know what will appeal to your friends. It is better to do something simple but do it well than to over-reach and find that you don't have the resources to make it work.

Please note: Ensure that the launch event is consistent with the style and ambience that you will create for the rest of your course. You don't want to get everyone there to a loud, fun launch night, only to have a quiet discussion the following week.

2 WHO IS GOING TO HELP US?

You will probably want to ask the team who are helping you to plan your Youth Alpha course to get involved, but feel free to ask if others are willing to help out with this one-time event. Get together early to brainstorm ideas, and make a plan for what you are going to do.

3 WHERE WILL WE HOLD OUR LAUNCH EVENT?

There are two options to consider here. The first option is to use the same venue for the Launch Event as you will use for your course. This will ensure that your guests are familiar with the venue from the start of the course, and it will mean that it is easier for them to find, as they will have been there before.

The other option, however, is to use a venue that you otherwise wouldn't use and to do something bigger and better—giving your event the "wow" factor (it may also be impractical to have a five-a-side football tournament in your living room).

Either way, don't forget to book the venue early!

4 WHAT SORT OF ENTERTAINMENT DO WE WANT?

Obviously the entertainment you book will depend on the type of event you intend to have. Once this decision has been made, start making arrangements as soon as you can. This may include booking a DJ, band, etc.

5 HOW WILL WE ADVERTISE OUR EVENT?

Be creative with how you advertise your event. There are all the "old school" ideas such as fliers, posters, and invitations, but you should also use media-related methods—create a *Facebook* event, make a video that you can post on *YouTube* or that you can send by text message. Have fun with your advertising! Make as much "noise" as you can.

6 HOW MUCH WILL IT COST?

Just as you made a budget for your course, so we would advise you to do the same for the Launch Event—start by trying to figure out how much everything will cost. You could ask people for a donation as they arrive, but it is even better if your event can be free. In order to ensure that this is possible, you may want to ask your church for financial help.

PLANNING YOUR YOUTH ALPHA WEEKEND OR DAY

The Youth Alpha Weekend or Day is one of the most important parts of Youth Alpha. Even if you aren't able to run a whole weekend, covering the Holy Spirit material is vital to the success of the course.

If there is one piece of advice that we would give you, it is that you should have a Weekend or Day as part of your course. If this seems daunting, then you can always ask your youth pastor or Youth Alpha Advisor for help in organizing it. In some cases, it may be possible for you to join another course's Weekend/Day, providing they are fairly local.

Why is the Weekend/Day so vital? It is the only part of the course that includes teaching on the person and work of the Holy Spirit. It also gives those on the course the chance to be prayed for and filled with the Holy Spirit. Our experience is that the Weekend/Day is the most fun part of the course, and it is also the time when relationships are formed in a much deeper way. We are sure that if you run a weekend you'll never look back!

There are, however, some very good, practical reasons why it may not be possible to run a weekend. These include:

Financial reasons – as we have said earlier, we don't want anyone to be excluded from any part of Youth Alpha because they can't afford it. Therefore, you need to decide in advance whether you have the resources to help those that can't afford to pay the full amount, and if not, it is probably a better idea to go for the cheaper day option, as this will be accessible to everyone.

Practical – if you are running a course on your own without the support of an adult team, you may find there are legal reasons why you can't run a weekend—i.e.: you don't have any guardians who are over eighteen to supervise the group.

Contextual – if you are running a course in a school it is probably not appropriate to expect the students to go away with you for a weekend. It may be a better idea to incorporate the Holy Spirit material into the weekly sessions.

Relational – if your course will include youth who don't know you well, they (and/or their parents) may be unsure about the idea of going away for a weekend with you. Some will have very genuine concerns that our motives may not be good. Questions like, "Will my child be brainwashed or inducted into some cult?" might seem slightly funny to us, but could be a real concern for many. Obviously, we should do all we can to dispel such fears by being open in all our planning and communication with parents and guardians, but we might have to accept that a weekend away is simply too much to ask for some.

If you decide that having a weekend away is not the right thing to do, you can still plan a Youth Alpha Day.

PLANNING – STAGE 1 (3–6 months in advance)

THINGS TO CONSIDER

1. WHEN DO WE RUN THE WEEKEND/DAY?

2. WHERE DO WE RUN IT?

3. HOW DO WE AFFORD IT?

4. HOW WILL WE GET THERE?

5. HOW DO WE TRAIN OUR TEAM?

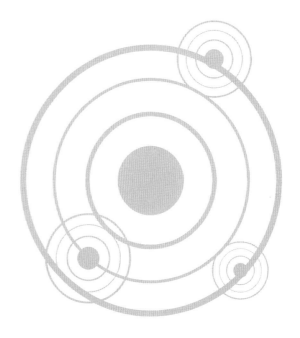

1 WHEN DO WE RUN THE WEEKEND/DAY?

Ideally, the Youth Alpha Weekend or Day should take place some time between week five and week eight of the course. This is roughly at the halfway point. By this time, the guests will have heard about various aspects of the Christian faith, including prayer, the Bible, the cross, and so on. Hopefully they will have had some good small group discussions and developed friendships and trust with others in the group.

As you choose the date for your weekend, bear in mind possible clashes: vacations, big school events like fairs or plays, birthday parties, and important sporting occasions that you know the group won't want to miss.

2 WHERE DO WE RUN IT?

This is an important decision, and there are resources available to help you find venues that cater for groups of young people. If in doubt, *Google* it!

One key consideration is obviously cost. It is wonderful to go to a purpose-built youth venue with state of the art media and facilities for outdoor activities, but if this is going to make it too expensive for some of your group then it will defeat the object.

A well-planned, well-run weekend with people sleeping on camping mattresses on the floor of a church hall (or similar) can be just as effective, and in some ways, even more memorable. Think about what the needs and desires of your group will be, and try to match that with what they will be able to afford.

You have much greater flexibility if you are planning a day. Although you won't be able to go too far (nor do you need to), it may still be a good idea to get off site and go somewhere new. Think creatively: why not ask a church across town if you can borrow a meeting room? Or ask a member of your church if you can use their home?

3 HOW DO WE AFFORD IT?

As we have said many times, we want the Youth Alpha Weekend/Day to be available to everyone on the course, regardless of how much they can afford. You may choose to set a price for the weekend, but if you have the financial resources (or the offer of subsidy from others), you could make it very cheap, or give people the option to pay only what they can afford. This is left to your discretion. It is our experience that speaking to your church about Youth Alpha's vision is really helpful, as church members may well want to sponsor individuals to go on the weekend.

4 HOW WILL WE GET THERE?

Depending on the size of your course and the desired location of the Weekend or Day, it may be possible to use the cars of adult leaders, if they have them. However, if the group is likely to be large, you will need to hire other transportation and this must be booked well in advance. If you want to keep costs down, it might be worth approaching other churches, youth organizations, or a local authority to see if you can find a cheap rental before you go direct to private rental firms or coach companies.

Please note: no financial saving is worth any kind of compromise on safety. You must consider all vehicles, drivers, and insurance arrangements carefully before committing to anything.

5 HOW DO WE TRAIN OUR TEAM?

The second Youth Alpha team training session is called "How to pray for each other on Youth Alpha." It is essential to do this before the Weekend/Day, as this is the first time that the team will be offering to pray for each member of the group. Training in this is vital, even for those who think they know enough already. The talk outline for this training session can be found on page 91 in Section 3.

PLANNING – STAGE 2 (1–2 months in advance)

THINGS TO CONSIDER

1. WHAT DO WE DO ON THE WEEKEND/DAY?
2. HOW DO WE PROMOTE IT?
3. DO WE NEED PERMISSION?

1 WHAT DO WE DO ON THE WEEKEND/ DAY?

The program for your Weekend/Day should be worked out between one and two months in advance. This will give you plenty of time to put all of your ideas into practice, resulting in an unforgettable weekend for your group! You will find some very basic sample programs for a Youth Alpha Weekend/ Day in Appendix 3 on page 107, or online at alphausa.org/youthdownloads.

These are intended to get you thinking about what might work well for your group in the venue you have booked.

Some general points to note

Worship – you may or may not have included worship as part of your course up until now. For some groups, the Youth Alpha Weekend will be the first time that worship is introduced, so it is worth putting a lot of effort into it. Worship is a great corporate activity, and it really helps to bring people into the presence of God.

Afternoon activities – in the afternoon, you may want to give your groups free time, or you may prefer to organize some sports/group games. If you are at a venue that offers instructed activities, this is a great option. If you are running a Youth Alpha Day, a great way to make the afternoon special is to plan a fun group activity that everyone will enjoy.

Evening session – if you are on a weekend away, you can hold the evening session either before or after dinner. In some ways, this is the most important talk of the whole course, so it may be a good thing to do it before dinner when people are more alert. After a meal we can feel lethargic and sleepy, but people's hunger may outweigh that—you should make the call based on your group.

Prayer ministry – it is important to note that on Youth Alpha we never ask people to respond to a "call" for prayer by raising their hand, or coming forward—we simply offer to pray for everyone. It is a good idea to have group leaders sitting with their groups so they can easily offer prayer to each person. There should be no pressure on anyone to be prayed for. If you are running a weekend, we suggest having another time of ministry on Sunday after the talk.

Talks – there are three talks included for use on the weekend. The third talk, "How Can I Make the Most of the Rest of My Life?" will probably not fit into a single day program, so could be done either at the next Youth Alpha session, or at the end of the course.

2 HOW DO WE PROMOTE IT?

We recommend that you start talking about the Weekend/Day on the second session of the course. The Weekend/Day will be an exciting time, but some people may feel intimidated by the idea of it on the first week. You should aim to have a flier, booking form, and parents' information sheet available for your guests by week two or three of the course. We would suggest mentioning the Weekend/Day at every session, and during the two sessions before your Weekend/Day, ask your small group leaders to encourage their groups to come.

As with the course invitation and Launch Event, you could use media such as videos and social networking sites to create a "buzz" about the Youth Alpha Weekend or Day.

3 DO WE NEED PERMISSION?

With teenagers under eighteen it is vital to get permission from their parents/guardians before you can take them anywhere. In Appendix 4 (page 109) of this *Leaders' Guide* you will find a sample parents' information sheet/booking form. An amendable copy of this form can be found at alphausa.org/ youthdownloads, which you can adapt and use to ensure that all parents/guardians are aware of your arrangements. Anyone who does not have permission from a parent/guardian cannot attend the Youth Alpha Weekend/Day. In the US, please follow the federal and state laws that apply to Child Protection. Including background checks for adult helpers. Please see the article, "Staying safe on Youth Alpha" on page 64. You should also ensure that at least one of your leaders/team is certified in first aid.

For your Youth Alpha Weekend/Day, we recommend a minimum of one adult for every six under eighteen year olds.

PLANNING – STAGE 3 (2–4 months in advance)

1. WHAT DO WE NEED TO TAKE ON OUR WEEKEND/DAY?

2. WHAT INFORMATION SHOULD WE GIVE OUT?

3. WHO IS DOING WHAT?

1 WHAT DO WE NEED TO TAKE ON OUR WEEKEND/DAY?

You should consult with the venue to figure out what you need to bring. Ask things like:

- Is any bedding provided? What about towels?

- Do you have a DVD player/computer/TV/projector we can use?

- What sports facilities are there?

- What cleaning duties do we need to do?

- Who cooks/what cooking facilities are there?

It's also a good idea to take a stack of Bibles with you.

2 WHAT INFORMATION SHOULD WE GIVE OUT?

It is useful to put together a pack for everyone who is coming on the Youth Alpha Weekend or Day. It should include all of the information they will need, such as a list of what they should bring, exact details of where and when everyone is meeting, how they will travel, and exactly when and where they will be dropped off when the weekend or day is over.

You'll also want to make sure that the parents of your group are really well informed about the Youth Alpha Weekend/Day. We suggest you put together a pack for parents, including the venue details and contact numbers (both for the venue and your group leaders), a timetable, and the parents' information sheet/booking form—see Appendix 4 on page 109 for samples of these. Amendable versions of these sheets and forms can be found online at alphausa.org/youthdownloads.

3 WHO IS DOING WHAT?

Make sure that your team are clear about who is doing what on the weekend/day. Well in advance, you should decide who is speaking, and, if you plan on having worship you should decide who will lead it.

In some cases, you may feel like you need some extra support and expertise on your Youth Alpha Weekend or Day. You might like to invite a guest speaker, a guest worship leader, or another type of specialist to help with a particular part of the weekend/day. A local Youth Alpha Advisor might be able to help with some recommendations if you don't already have the contacts. Such people tend to be busy, though, and you will need to book them well in advance. The only thing to be mindful of is that it usually takes time for young people to develop trust—before you invite a guest, ensure you are confident that the group will not feel threatened by having someone new come into their midst.

We suggest giving one person the responsibility of hosting the sessions and making announcements, etc., for the whole weekend/day, so it is clear to everyone that someone is in charge.

You can also assign responsibilities to others on your team for:

- Catering (if not taken care of by the venue)

- Entertainment (organizing a talent show or similar?)

- Games and ice breakers

- Sports and activities

PLANNING – STAGE 4 (1 week in advance)

THINGS TO CONSIDER

1. WHERE WILL PEOPLE SLEEP?

2. DOES THE VENUE HAVE ALL THE INFORMATION THEY NEED?

3. HAVE I GOT EVERYTHING PLANNED AND WRITTEN DOWN?

1 WHERE WILL PEOPLE SLEEP?

It is much better to draw up a bedroom plan for the weekend before you leave rather than trying to do it upon arrival. This can be a work of art in itself—but just remember that you can't please everybody all of the time.

A few hints

- Try to keep small groups together as much as you can.

- It might be helpful to put girls and guys in separate areas of the venue, e.g., on different floors if appropriate.

- Try to spread leaders and other trusted individuals around the venue evenly to keep things calm.

2 DOES THE VENUE HAVE ALL THE INFORMATION THEY NEED?

Make a call to the venue to give them final numbers for rooms/catering (if appropriate) and let them know what time you will arrive, etc.

3 DO YOU HAVE EVERYTHING PLANNED AND WRITTEN DOWN?

Making sure you have everything written down is really important, especially if you are going off site. We would suggest you draw up a master list that includes:

- The name of each person who is coming

- Any allergies, medical, or dietary requirements

- Parents'/guardians' names and contact details

- Contact details for each person's doctor, as well as contact details for a local doctor

- How each person is travelling to and from the venue (which car, train, bus, etc.)

- Whether they have paid and what they owe

- Which room they will sleep in

- Which small group they are in

- Any duties they are assigned to (for leaders/ helpers only)

- A separate list of what equipment you need to bring (including the required equipment for talk illustrations)

Finally, after all of your planning and preparation, don't forget to pray. Enjoy your Youth Alpha Weekend or Day and watch God move!

PLANNING YOUR FOLLOW-UP

Before you begin running a Youth Alpha course, it is worth giving some thought to what will happen at the end of your course.

Jesus' commission to us is to "make disciples," not just converts. Follow-up after a Youth Alpha course is vital, and we need to be willing to commit to that before starting a course.

There are, of course, many different ways to follow-up from Youth Alpha. If you are part of a local church and/or youth group then it may be that your Youth Alpha group can easily join up with one or both of these. Certain denominations will have programs that help new Christians join their particular church.

It is important that you continue to be a part of everyone's journey, not just those in the group who have made a commitment to Jesus. It has been said many times that faith is a journey, and this journey doesn't start or end on Youth Alpha. If we suddenly stop talking to someone because they didn't make a decision for Jesus on our course, then that doesn't speak a great deal about our love for them.

Keep praying for your group and make arrangements to get together fairly regularly. Involve them in your church and invite them to your youth group. Your church or youth group may need to adapt slightly in order to make services/meetings more accessible to young people who are new to the Christian faith—this is not always easy to address, but these conversations are always very healthy.

Keep your eyes open for any practical needs that your friends may have in order to continue their journey. For example, do they have a Bible that they can read? Is there an appropriate Bible reading guide you can get them? Can you start a follow-up or discipleship group so that you can all continue meeting together in a similar context?

> *"Therefore go and make disciples of all nations, baptizing them in the name of the Father and of the Son and of the Holy Spirit, and teaching them to obey everything I have commanded you. And surely I am with you always, to the very end of the age" (Matthew 28:19-20)*

There are many Christian organizations that have produced great youth resources which could be used as follow-up programs to Youth Alpha. Visit alphausa.org/youth for links and information.

One great way of engaging people in the journey of faith is to invite some of those who did the last Youth Alpha course to come and help you run the next one. Why not ask them to be involved as small group leaders, speakers, or behind-the-scenes helpers? We've seen many cases where returning to help on a course has sparked someone's faith more than when they attended the course as a guest.

SECTION 2

EXPERT ADVICE ON RUNNING YOUTH ALPHA

HOW TO LEAD A YOUTH ALPHA SMALL GROUP

By Matt Costley

The British band Coldplay wrote a song called "Square One." It goes like this: "From the top of the first page/To the end of the last day/From the start in your own way/You just want somebody listening to what you say/It doesn't matter who you are."

I think these words pretty much sum up the way a lot of our generation feel about life. We just want to know that someone cares about what we have to say.

> We have one golden rule in small groups: no question is too simple or too hostile

Over recent years, we've seen a massive rise in the use of social networking and media-sharing websites such as *Facebook*, *Twitter*, *MySpace* and *YouTube* (to name a few). One of the reasons that so many of us are using them is that they affirm the idea that "my life matters" and that "the rest of the world needs to hear what I am doing and thinking."

On Youth Alpha, we want to make time to hear what everyone on the course thinks and feels. We believe that their life and their opinion do matter, even if we don't agree with them. We want to use the course to get to know each other and to build relationships. That's why, in many ways, small groups on Youth Alpha are the most important part of the whole course.

AIMS OF SMALL GROUPS

There are two main aims of small groups—to discuss, and to build relationships.

1 TO DISCUSS

On the first week of one of the courses I was involved in, a thirteen-year-old guy in my small group came out with a well-presented, three-point argument for why there was no God. I was impressed—he sounded like he knew what he was talking about. Someone asked him how he had come to those conclusions, and he froze. He repeated the same argument. Again, someone asked why he believed this, but he couldn't explain it. It turned out that he had learnt the three points from a teacher at school, but he didn't really understand what they meant.

In many ways, this is what the church has done to young people for years—we have given the "answers" without helping people to figure out *why* they are the answers.

It's important on your Youth Alpha course that you don't just feed people information, but that you give them time to find the answers for themselves. If we allow this to happen, then the fruit will be long-lasting and life-changing, rather than short-term and shallow.

John 16:13 says, "But when he, the Spirit of truth, comes, he will guide you into all truth." Discussion helps truth to rise to the surface, making it easier for everyone to discover for themselves. Talking together in a small group allows everyone to express their opinions. We don't need to be afraid of questions— actually, we embrace them. As that verse says, the Spirit will lead us into truth, and if something is true, it will stand up to any amount of questioning. We have one golden rule in small groups: no question is too simple or too hostile. In fact, the first time you get together in your group, it can be a good thing to identify in your head who the most hostile person might be and invite them to speak first— this will give permission to others to be honest too.

2 TO BUILD RELATIONSHIPS

When I first moved to London I didn't know a single person. Soon after I arrived, I did an Alpha course at my church and, during that time, became good friends with the people in my group. Eleven years later, those guys are still my best friends and we are doing life together.

Someone once said that people go to church for many reasons, but only come back for one—if they make friends. Hopefully the people in your small group will really enjoy hanging out and getting to know each other better. This aspect of the Youth Alpha course is so important; it's essential to spend time getting to know each other and letting friendships form.

FIVE TOP TIPS FOR SUCCESSFUL SMALL GROUPS

1 LEADERS ARE THERE TO FACILITATE DISCUSSION

Remember that the role of the small group leader is not so much to try to answer people's questions as it is to facilitate discussion. The best thing a leader can do is ask questions. A great one is, "So what do the rest of you think?" When someone offers a thought, it's not the leader's job to jump in with their own views or an answer, but instead to throw it open to the rest of the group.

The small group leaders on Youth Alpha are more like group facilitators than instructional gurus. A facilitator is simply another member of the group who is helping to keep the discussion going. Our views are no more important than anyone else's, and we are not looking to judge people or their opinions. It is our aim to guide and steer the group, so ask lots of questions!

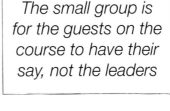

The small group is for the guests on the course to have their say, not the leaders

2 THEY'VE ALREADY HEARD A TALK

This is a key point to grasp. Remember that by the time we get to the small group time, everyone has already heard a talk—they don't want to hear another one. So any kind of preaching is banned! This can be really hard, especially if you are listening to people ask questions that you think are really easy to answer. You might be in a group where it seems that they have just managed to disprove all of Christianity—even so, don't try and defend it. The small group is for the guests on the course to have their say, not the leaders.

3 LOOK FOR OPINIONS NOT ANSWERS

Try to avoid asking closed questions—questions that have either "yes" or "no" as an answer. Instead, ask open-ended questions that require an opinion for an answer. Not only will this help to keep the discussion flowing, but it also means that there can be no right or wrong answer. A good thing to ask is, "What do you think/how do you feel about that?" as this makes it a more personal question.

There are lots of suggested questions listed at the end of the course sessions—feel free to use these if they are helpful for getting discussion going.

4 VALUE EVERY OPINION

Don't take sides in your group's discussion, but value every opinion that is shared. Even if someone says something that seems crazy or ridiculous, we want them to know that what they think matters to the group. You could say something like, "That's interesting. What does everybody else think?" This allows you to affirm them without having to agree, and it gives others in the group a chance to respond for themselves.

5 DON'T BE AFRAID TO LOSE THE ARGUMENT

This is one of the hardest things to do and it may go against every fiber of your being, but it is really important. We won't and don't have to "win" every discussion, sometimes it is better to lose! I have seen groups tear apart everything that was said in a talk, but still return week after week to hear the next topic. Many of the people in these groups came to faith because they had been given space to discuss things. We need to trust that if truth is truth, it will always come out.

DOS AND DON'TS

DON'T

- Ask a question and then answer it yourself. This devalues the question you have just asked

- Put somebody else's answer into your own words: it invalidates their explanation

- Be afraid to gently challenge or tease out a response, e.g.: "Can you explain what you mean by that?" or "Can you give an example?"

- Be afraid of silence. Allow time for the group to think about questions/issues raised. Allowing silence shows that you value thoughtful and considered responses. Someone will talk eventually!

DO

- Think about your group as you prepare your questions. Make the questions as relevant to them as possible

- Affirm responses neutrally, if possible, e.g.: "Yes" or "Thank you." This shows that you welcome further responses from others

- Answer questions with questions

GROUND RULES FOR YOUR SMALL GROUP

The last thing anyone wants is for their small group to feel like school, but it can be helpful to set some group ground rules on the first week to make sure everyone has a good time. Here are four that might help you:

1 NO PUT-DOWNS
We want everyone to respect each other. It's okay for the group to attack ideas, but not each other.

2 THERE'S NO SUCH THING AS A STUPID QUESTION
We want everyone to know it's okay to ask *any* question without being laughed at.

3 NO ONE HAS TO TALK, BUT ONLY ONE PERSON TALKS AT A TIME
We won't force anyone to speak, but we do want to respect each other and that means listening to what others have to say without talking over them.

4 WHAT IS SAID IN THE GROUP STAYS IN THE GROUP
If someone shares something personal in the group, there needs to be an understanding that it is not going to be passed on to others at school or anywhere else.

Lastly, don't forget to have fun in your groups, and always make sure that you finish on time or early —it's better to leave people wanting more than not wanting to come back because they got bored. If someone doesn't come back, don't worry—it's unlikely to be your fault. Keep praying for them anyway.

My experience is that being part of a Youth Alpha small group is by far the best element of the course—the friendships formed in those groups can last a lifetime.

> *We need to trust that if truth is truth, it will always come out*

Matt Costley is the Youth Pastor at Holy Trinity Brompton in London, and is the former Head of Youth Alpha.

htb.org.uk

HOW TO GIVE A GREAT YOUTH ALPHA TALK

By Gavin Calver

Leonard Sweet, an American writer and theologian, suggests that communicating to today's teenagers requires us to be **EPIC**:

Experiential – let them experience God.
Participatory – let them participate in the talk.
Image-driven – our talks should be image-heavy: whether in the form of movies, *YouTube* clips, pictures or images described using words (stories), teenagers respond to images.
Connected – we must be community centered (small groups).

[Adapted from Leonard Sweet, *Postmodern Pilgrims* (Broadman & Holman Publishers, 2000).]

The thing I love about Youth Alpha is that it lends itself to being EPIC. The opportunity to communicate the gospel in a way that our friends will understand is very exciting, but also challenging. On Youth Alpha, all the talks are given live—there is no fallback DVD option! Your aim is to bring out the session's subject with the help of video clips, icebreakers, and other creative aids.

Preparing and presenting a live talk every week can initially seem daunting, but it's actually one of the real strengths of Youth Alpha. Live talks help you to gauge exactly where your group are at week by week, helping you tailor the way you present the material to them. My aim here is to share some practical advice that may be helpful to consider before you start your Youth Alpha course. The real key is to prepare properly and to pray.

MAKE IT SHORT

Whatever else you do, always know exactly how you will start and finish your talk. It can be helpful to try to remember the first and last few sentences of your talk so that you can start and end confidently. Be incredibly disciplined about keeping to your allotted time, no matter how tempting it may be to run over.

The typical Youth Alpha guest doesn't have a huge attention span. Think of it a bit like a TV program —TV producers know we concentrate better in small bursts, so they use commercial breaks to split programs into more manageable chunks. Likewise, try to make your points quickly, using an illustration to break up the presentation and keep the group's attention. Use plenty of the suggested illustrations and do all you can to keep your young people engaged.

If you have had experience of speaking at an adult Alpha course, you now have to think shorter, shorter and even shorter. This can be hard; it seems easier to explain "Why Did Jesus Die?" in forty-five minutes, than to explain it in fifteen or twenty minutes. However, twenty minutes is actually quite a long time, and this should be seen as the absolute maximum talk length on Youth Alpha.

The better prepared you are, the shorter your talk will be—the less prepared you are, the more you will waffle! Why not ask a friend to listen to your talk beforehand and get them to offer suggestions?

MAKE IT MEMORABLE

Make use of illustrations, media clips and examples. The ones listed in this resource are great, but do not feel constrained by them. If you have other ideas that are suitable, use them instead (and share them online so other leaders can use them too).

> *On Youth Alpha, all the talks are given live—there is no fallback DVD option!*

> *The better prepared you are, the shorter your talk will be*

Make use of simple words and expressions that your group will understand. Don't use "Christian-speak" that those in the church may be used to. If you have to use "Christian" words like "redemption," "grace," "sin," "blood," and "repentance," explain them so that everyone understands their meaning.

Be yourself. Don't try to be something you're not. Your group will see straight through it. Be true to your personality: don't try and be funny if it doesn't come naturally to you. People respect authenticity, so be genuine without being too heavy or intense. Remember, it's not about being cool—it's about loving people and drawing them closer to the kingdom of God.

Make use of the Bible, but don't expect the group to know anything about it. Assume that even the most common Bible stories are unknown to them. This can actually be a help, as hearing the stories for the first time often has a powerful impact on people.

MAKE IT PERSONAL

Make use of your own experiences in your talk. Personal stories are often the ones that young people remember afterwards, so these are an important part of the talk. You could also involve other leaders in sharing stories from their lives if they are relevant to the talk (make sure you check them beforehand). Don't underestimate the power of personal testimony. If we are vulnerable in our story telling then this can have a profound effect on a Youth Alpha group.

Don't forget that, whatever your age, you are a great example. The group may have forgotten what you said by next week, but they *will* remember what kind of person you are and how you live your life.

Sometimes you might not get much of a response from the group. That doesn't mean that you have given a bad talk (but do ask for feedback from your friends). My experience is that a lot can be happening in a person, even if they don't immediately respond to your words. The Holy Spirit works in people's hearts even if we can't see it. If we do our best, then God does the rest.

Gavin Calver is the National Director of British Youth for Christ.

yfc.co.uk

HOW TO PRAY FOR EACH OTHER ON YOUTH ALPHA

By Mike Pilavachi

When I first became a Christian I learned that Jesus didn't just *say* wonderful things, He also *demonstrated* wonderful things: He *taught* the good news and He *lived* the good news. I learned that part of what He did was to set people free by praying for them in various ways. Jesus' ministry of healing people and setting them free didn't end when He died and rose from the dead: He gave that ministry to His church, to His people.

For a while, the only group prayer I had ever seen modelled involved lining up in front of a few super-spiritual Christians on a stage and waiting to receive prayer. I thought that if these people (they usually wore white suits and spoke in American accents) prayed for me I'd be blessed, but if a neighbor or someone sitting next to me at church prayed for me, well, that just wasn't the same.

A few years ago, I turned up at a church just outside London and I discovered that prayer isn't meant to be like that. At the time, I was really broken: a lot of things had gone wrong in my life. At the end of the service, the vicar (it was an Anglican church) said, "If anyone would like prayer for anything then come forward and the ministry team will come and pray for you." I was curious, as I'd never seen anything like this before.

People went forward, and the ministry team prayed for them in a really relaxed way. It looked so calm! Lots of different things seemed to happen—some were really obvious and some were less so. Some people started to cry, and at first I thought, "Oh no, they're upset, why isn't anyone comforting them?" Others started to laugh and I *really* didn't get that. Some people started to shake a little bit, and some people even seemed to fall down, which scared me the first few times. The next week, there were testimonies

from some of the people I had seen receiving prayer, and they would talk about the amazing things that God had done to them on the inside while they were being prayed for.

I realized that until that moment, I had only looked at what was happening on the outside, when all the while God had been working on the inside. My immediate thought was, "Wow, this ministry team are so holy and spiritual, I could never be like that."

I was desperate to meet with God, so regardless of what they asked people to go forward for, I'd go anyway! If the vicar asked if people wanted to respond to a call to be an evangelist, or a pastor, or to go to outer Mongolia as a missionary, I'd go forward to get prayed for. The amazing thing was, perhaps because I was desperate, God would meet with me, often in very real ways.

> *I thought, 'Oh no! I can't pray on my own, I'm not spiritual, I'm not holy, nothing will happen'*

I still stood in awe of the ministry team—I thought they were so spiritual and amazing. Then one Sunday night, the vicar said to me, "Mike, I'd like you to join the ministry team." I thought, "The man's an idiot! He doesn't know what I'm really like; he doesn't realize that I'm not spiritual," so I said okay before he found out and changed his mind.

I started out by praying in a "tag team" with a more experienced man from church (probably to prevent me killing anyone by mistake). We prayed for people, but I really believed it was the other guy's prayers that counted, not mine.

One Sunday, there were loads of people wanting prayer. The person leading the ministry said, "Mike, we don't have enough people to pray, you're going to have to pray on your own tonight." I thought, "Oh no! I can't pray on my own, I'm not spiritual, I'm not holy, nothing will happen." I just panicked and hoped that the person I was going to pray for would only have something small, like a headache. The guy I went up to asked me to pray for two things: a bad back and really bad depression. I said, "Okay, let's pray for the depression first" (I chose this because I thought it would be harder to tell whether or not he was healed. That way he wouldn't notice that my prayers didn't work). I put my hand on his shoulder, and said some words. Inside I was thinking, "Oh go on Lord, please. Just this once. I'll do anything, even be nice to my sister," but outside I was trying to look very spiritual. I thought I'd pray for a short time and then explain why sometimes people don't get healed.

Suddenly, the guy opened his eyes and said, "That's amazing—my depression's lifted, I feel like I can laugh for the first time in ages!" I tried to look very confident, as if I'd expected that and I said, "Shall we go for the double and pray for your back too?" I put my hand on his back and prayed inside my head, "Go on, go on Lord, do another one." After a while, he opened his eyes and said, "Thank you for praying for me." I thought, "That means his back's not healed." Still, I was pretty pleased, because one out of two ain't bad!

Later, I was talking to someone else when the same guy ran up and said, "Look, I've just realized I can do this," and he started doing all sorts of things with his body—his back was healed. I left that night walking on air. I suddenly realized a great truth: "I'm spiritual, I'm holy, I heal people," and I couldn't wait for next Sunday. The next week, I prayed for someone with great faith—I rebuked the disease, I blessed the person, I prayed quietly in a whisper and then I rose to a crescendo. When he opened his eyes, I said, "Well?" He replied, "Nothing's happened, except my legs hurt because I've been standing here for so long," and he left.

I was really confused. I thought, "God, last week when I didn't have much faith, you healed someone, but this week nothing! Why?" At that moment a verse of scripture came into my mind (it's in Proverbs, James, and 1 Peter): "God opposes the proud but gives grace

Praying for others is something we can all do

to the humble." At that point I knew exactly what it was all about.

Praying for others is something we can all do. It's not about people who think they are spiritual and holy or those who stand on platforms. This is a ministry for the whole body of Christ, for the whole church—for everybody. The people God loves to use the most seem to be the people that know that they can't do it on their own. They know that if God doesn't show up, they're in trouble.

One of the things I love about Youth Alpha is that it gives people on the course the chance to be prayed for. This first happens on the Youth Alpha Weekend or Day, and later in the course, during the session on healing. In our groups, we want to model how to pray for each other in a simple way that is easily replicable. This will show people that they, too, can begin to pray for others. While there may be 300 different ways to pray for someone, I want to give you a really simple model that all of us can use, regardless of experience.

FOUR VALUES OF PRAYER MINISTRY

I want to suggest four values we should hold on to as we pray for people:

1 WE VALUE THE CROSS OF JESUS CHRIST
The death of Jesus Christ on the cross is central to everything. Everything we receive is because of the cross, not because of us. At the foot of the cross, we are all the same size; we're all the same. This helps us realize that it's not about you or me, and it's not about an "anointed" person who comes to town—it's about the anointed person who is Jesus.

It's His anointing, His gifts, His power; it all comes from Him and it's all because of the cross. If we value the cross of Jesus Christ, we realize that the ultimate and best healing is forgiveness—coming into relationship with Him: that's the root of everything else. When we value the cross of Jesus we don't pray prayers like this, "Lord, bless and heal Jane because she is such a good person and she really deserves it." Instead we will pray, "Lord, bless and heal Jane because You are such a wonderful God, because You've already done it and You've already earned it.' We value the cross of Christ and that puts everything else in its place.

2 WE VALUE THE BIBLE AS THE WORD OF GOD

The Bible is our final authority on all matters of faith and conduct. That doesn't mean that there aren't other authorities, but these all fall under the final authority, which is God's Word. That means the way we pray needs to come under the scrutiny of Scripture and conform to what the Bible says.

We sometimes hear bizarre stories about what God is doing. If we value the Bible as God's Word, we take those stories we hear, and we check them with the book. There's certainly enough bizarre stuff *in* the Bible to keep us going for ages before we need to start looking for bizarre stuff *outside* it! Like Jesus spitting on mud and rubbing the paste in a man's eyes to heal him—what's that about?

Yet Jesus Christ is our model for ministry as revealed in the Bible, so we've got to be people of the book; people who read and study the Bible.

3 WE VALUE THE PERSON AND WORK OF THE HOLY SPIRIT

What does that mean? That means it is *His* work and not ours. Actually, that is amazing news—we are released from the burden of feeling like *we* have to do something. It's God that does it, not us. When we're praying for people, we need to look at ourselves like waiters and

> *When we're praying for people, we need to look at ourselves like waiters and waitresses in a restaurant*

waitresses in a restaurant. The customer comes in, and we go up to them and say, "What is your order, Sir/Madam?" They may say, "A bad left knee, healed please." We write down, "Bad left knee healed," and we take the order to the chef. Only the chef can make up the order, and in the same way, only God does the healing.

We get to be involved, we get to be waiters and waitresses, but Jesus does the healing—He does it with us. That's great news: if it's God's work and not ours, we don't need to stress, just keep it simple.

4 WE VALUE THE DIGNITY OF THE INDIVIDUAL

It's really important that we treat people with respect and dignity, just as we would like to be treated. If we are praying for someone, the worst thing we can do is get distracted and stop concentrating, that is not affirming and valuing an individual.

The ultimate goal is that the people we pray for meet with Jesus. Sometimes when we pray, it will all seem very gentle. At other times, it might be less gentle—people may laugh or cry, shake or fall over. All of this is okay, we respect their dignity.

PRACTICAL TIPS

We always encourage guys to pray with guys and girls to pray with girls. This just makes it easier for people to be honest with each other. We all know there will be some things guys wouldn't want to talk about in front of girls and vice versa.

First of all, **invite** the Holy Spirit to come. The Holy Spirit has been there the whole time, but now we're asking Him to bring His presence to the person we're praying for. We can pray three words: "Come Holy Spirit."

The trick then is to **wait**. The temptation is to cover the silence with words—sometimes we find silence embarrassing—but actually, we just need to wait for the Lord.

Then we **watch**. We can keep our eyes open: in Biblical times they prayed with their eyes open. Jesus told the disciples to "watch and pray" (Matthew 26:41). Jesus said, "I only do what I see my Father doing, I only speak the words my Father gives me to speak." This means, "I want to follow Him, I want to see what He is doing and I want to join in with that."

The ultimate goal is that the people we pray for meet with Jesus

I wasted many years of my Christian life saying to God, "Lord, this is what I want to do, would you bless that?" It's actually much more fun to find out what God's already doing and just joining in with that—it takes the stress away.

Sometimes the first thing that the person receiving prayer feels is a sense of peace. Then, really calmly, you may want to pray. If, for example, it's a bad left shoulder you are praying for, just put your hand gently on the shoulder and ask for healing in Jesus' name: "Lord would you bring healing here." You don't need to do anything weird, just keep watching and waiting. Often, you don't see anything happening, and yet the person gets healed.

I want to remind you to only lay your hands on appropriate parts of the body (I won't go into details about this!). The only way to get better at praying for people in these ways is by doing it, so try!

When you have finished praying, you can ask what happened. If they say, "Actually, I don't think anything happened," do not respond by saying, "Nothing?! That's odd. You're the tenth person I've prayed for tonight and all the others were miraculously healed and set free. What's wrong with you?" If we treat people like that, they will leave discouraged. We should simply encourage people that God's Spirit always comes when we ask Him, but we don't always sense what He is doing.

Praying for each other on Youth Alpha is an opportunity to cooperate with God and bless others with *His* blessing. It's not something reserved for only a few people—it's for all of us.

Mike Pilavachi is the Founder and Director of Soul Survivor.

soulsurvivor.com

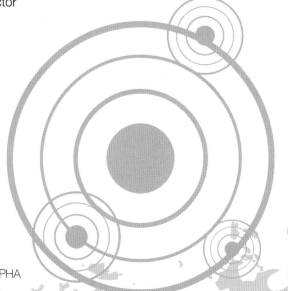

PRAYING FOR YOUR YOUTH ALPHA COURSE

By Pete Greig

Well, it's been a long, slow process, but recently I got converted. Evangelists have been telling me for ages how much better my life will be if I see things the way they do. They've explained that I won't fully understand until I take the leap of faith, and they've testified to their own personal experiences. In the end I'm not sure if I was won over, or merely ground down. Anyway, I finally did it: I upgraded my battered old cell phone for a sleek black iPhone.

To be honest, my old phone really wasn't that bad. If you want to see a bad phone, you should check out the one my mom uses on the Isle of Wight. It's the size of a brick, and at times, she has to stand on one leg on the front doorstep, with the phone about twelve inches from her ear just to make the wretched thing work. Compared to hers, my old cell was fine, so I guess I was a reluctant convert.

Despite the fact there have been no blinding lights and no angelic choirs, now I've made the switch I must admit that my iPhone really is better. I'm even telling my friends about it, and I actually caught myself advertising an Apple course at the church of All Things Apple.

My old phone was functional, but my iPhone is fun too. What's more (bear with me here), it's actually taught me things about communicating with God. My prayer life can easily become merely formal and functional, when it's meant to be fascinating, enjoyable, intuitive, and expansive.

What I'm realizing more and more is that prayer isn't just a way of getting things done and making things happen (a healing here, a heavenly memo there, and a parking space at the supermarket on a Saturday afternoon). Prayer is the life-giving heartbeat of a

> *Prayer isn't just a way of getting things done and making things happen*

dynamic, colorful, intuitive, intelligent, fun interaction with Jesus Christ.

When he was very little, my son Danny came into my study one day and started playing with my hole-punch. He was very taken with it, very impressed, and he spent a long time driving it around the floor like a car and snapping it like a crocodile. It was a long time before he turned to me and said, "Daddy, what is this for?"

We can often treat our faith like that— enjoying it, admiring it, using it for all sorts of things but never really stopping to wonder, "Father, what is it for? Why have I been saved? What is the point? Now that I am Spirit-filled, baptized, and helping on a Youth Alpha course—what now?"

I sometimes wonder what Adam and Eve talked about with God every evening in the Garden of Eden before the Fall. After all, there was no sin to fight, no sickness to heal, no Gospel to preach, no transformation of society required. They didn't pray to make stuff happen, they prayed because they enjoyed sharing their lives with God—it was the most natural thing in the world. It was what they were made to do.

We are not Christians because of some cosmic strategy, and we do not pray merely to get things done while functionally serving the Lord. My wife Sammy and I did not have children as a "child-raising strategy," but as an expression of our intimacy: we desired to lovingly raise children to maturity. We pray because we're wired for delightful intimacy with God.

I'm so excited that you're setting out on this journey of running a Youth Alpha course. I would encourage you to simply find a friend or two and get together to pray for your course. It's a good thing to pray for the course in the months and weeks leading up to it, as well as throughout the course itself. Ask others to pray for you and your course, too. If you ask God to do specific things, you'll be amazed at the miracles you'll see!

There are no secrets to this stuff, but I would encourage you to try to make it fun as well as functional. Why not include worship, or write down, draw, or paint your prayers, or maybe use some visual aids such as photos as you pray for people. Try sticking your small group list on the bathroom mirror, or setting your phone alarm to remind you to pray a one-liner for them at a certain time each day? You can also visit www.24-7prayer.com for more ideas and encouraging stories, or get hold

of my book *Red Moon Rising* which will really help you get excited about the power of prayer.

Let's upgrade our prayer lives by daring to ask big things of God, and making prayer as creative and enjoyable as possible—the word "functional" only makes sense with those first three letters (fun!) at the start.

I hope that as you run Youth Alpha for your friends you also celebrate and grow in your relationship with God, by making time to walk and talk with Him each day. That is something my iPhone will never really help me with, but that's what I'm here for and that's all that really matters.

> *We pray because we're wired for delightful intimacy with God*

Pete Greig is one of the leaders of the 24-7 Prayer movement and is also Director of Prayer at Holy Trinity Brompton in London.

24-7prayer.com

USING MULTIMEDIA ON YOUTH ALPHA

By Phil Knox

There is a fascinating moment in the book of Acts when Paul is preaching the gospel in Athens. He notices an altar "to an unknown God" and basically says, "I know this God, he has a name, and his name is Jesus." Paul uses the things that are around him to communicate the good news in a way that people will understand.

Today we live in a multimedia-filled society. Technology is everywhere, and if Paul were communicating the gospel in the 21st century I am sure he would still be using things around him to help. So how do we make the most of this massive area of technology?

FILM CLIPS

Every Youth Alpha session contains a selection of film clips to choose from that will help you illustrate the message. They can be powerful, memorable, entertaining, and they can enhance your talk. Unfortunately, due to copyright restrictions, Youth Alpha cannot provide these film clips for you, so the first step is to decide which films you want to use, followed by borrowing or renting them.

Top tips

- Find and check video clips well in advance. Make sure they are appropriate. For more ideas (including films released since this resource was written), visit youthalpha.org

- Make sure the clip is cued, the sound level is right, and the lighting is adequate. Check the timecodes—we have done this for you in this resource, but in some DVD regions this may be out by several seconds

- Think carefully about how you will introduce and talk about the clip. Make sure you fill in the necessary background for those who have never seen the film but don't give away what happens altogether

- Don't feel you need to use a popular, recent film—sometimes a film the group haven't seen before can be more powerful in making the point

- Check that you have the right license to show movie clips—in the US, most churches and schools will have a license already. See www.ccli.com for information

---

> *For more ideas (including films released since this resource was written), visit youthalpha.org*

INTERNET VIDEO CLIPS

Internet videos, along with wireless Internet, have exploded in the last few years, meaning that the use of online videos has become a possibility in Youth Alpha sessions. To this end, we have included some links to relevant clips on our website (alphausa.org/youth).

Top tips

- There are several programs on the Internet that can help you download a *YouTube* video rather than streaming it—this can be useful, especially if there is no Internet access in your venue

- Make your own videos. This creates a great sense of ownership and community. *YouTube* is all about participating and contributing, even though the quality is not always that great. Get some of your team to film vox pops on the week's subject, or film a five minute mock documentary

- If you do make videos or find any good clips to use, share them online at youthalpha.org so others can access them

- It is worth noting that the terms and conditions of *YouTube* say that clips are licensed for private and personal use only. If you wish to show these clips to your youth group you should always seek permission to do so from the copyright holder

POWERPOINT

Powerpoint can be a great way of keeping attention and building momentum through a session. It helps people keep track of what they are learning, and can be especially useful as each Youth Alpha session has a number of clear points to communicate.

Top tips

- Make sure the text is big enough to read

- Use powerful images from the Internet. We live in an image-rich culture and our generation will engage better and remember more if there is a memorable image with each point. There are many websites offering free images such as www.freefoto.com

- Go through the presentation beforehand so you know it works and matches your talk

- Print off the order of your slides so you know what is coming next

MUSIC

Music can also be a great way of connecting with teenagers, and there may be some great tracks that really communicate a key point of a session.

Top tips

- Be aware that music, almost more than anything else, divides as well as unites. Be careful not to alienate half your group with choice of a particular style

Make your own videos. This creates a great sense of ownership and community

- If you use some contemporary Christian music, try to look at it through the eyes of a teenager who has no experience of Christian worship—is it relevant?

- Playing a whole four minute track may be too long to engage a group in just listening. Consider playing just part of a track, or using a visually rich Powerpoint presentation to accompany the music

PRACTICAL ADVICE

Make sure that your media will work when you want it to. The biggest piece of advice we can give you as a leader is to get someone else to help. There are loads of people who love technology, and this can be a great way of getting them involved in serving. Make sure you prepare adequately and fully brief the person you ask—it is well worth having a practice run through so they know when to play each clip.

Top tips

- If you are using a laptop to play a DVD, you can bookmark the scene you want—this means that it will remember where to start from even if you play another DVD first

- Factor in the amount of time it will take to change and cue the next DVD (if you're using more than one)

- Try not to cue up a DVD scene on screen while the speaker is talking—it will be distracting. If you can use another monitor, that is better

We are really passionate about exploring the meaning of life and communicating the good news in a relevant and accessible way. Technology is a great way of doing this. Have fun with using multimedia in your sessions; we hope they communicate the life-changing message of Jesus in a relevant way.

Phil Knox is the Evangelism Resources Senior Manager at British Youth for Christ.

yfc.co.uk

WORSHIP ON YOUTH ALPHA

By Al Gordon

Worship is key to what Alpha is all about—giving people the chance to meet Jesus. When I was eighteen, a friend gave me a tape of worship music that had been recorded at a gathering of about 10,000 young people. I remember putting the tape into my walkman (retro, I know), and being blown away by the presence of God that seemed to fill my bedroom. That was the first time I experienced the Holy Spirit, and I remain convinced of the importance of worship.

Surprisingly, perhaps, worship plays a central role in an Alpha course. The key question is, how on earth can you ask a bunch of people who don't believe that God exists to worship?

THE FATHER SEEKS WORSHIPERS

Evangelism is about restoring correct worship. Worship is one of those things that everyone does instinctively: it's a first order human activity, like breathing, eating, and sleeping. Jesus came to restore right worship so that everyone can find purpose and meaning in a loving relationship with their heavenly Father.

The Westminster Catechism says, "The chief end of man is to glorify God and enjoy him forever." At what point do we let people know this? When they've been hanging around church for a while? If our main purpose is to be worshipers, then worship must be at the heart of our gospel message: worship and evangelism go hand in hand.

WORSHIP DRAWS PEOPLE TO GOD

There's a brilliant story in Acts 16:25, where Paul and Silas have been thrown in jail for telling people about Jesus. They start worshiping, God intervenes supernaturally, the doors of the jail are blown off and

half of the prison is converted. Worship can have a powerful impact on people who don't know God, because He is present.

WORSHIP IS WHAT WE DO

We're the church. We worship. It's a fact. It's been this way from the start of our story. People know this about us and there's no point in pretending we don't worship. We do. Because we're the church.

When people come and hang out with us, wanting to find out a bit more about what we believe, we shouldn't start pretending that the things we really value aren't important to us. That would be lacking in authenticity.

> *Worship and evangelism go hand in hand*

We want our evangelism to give people a taste of what church is like, and "what-you-see-is-what-you-get" is a really important principle. We don't need to try and pretend we don't love to worship. We do, however, need to think about how we introduce people to worshiping Jesus, given that the whole worship-earthquake-chains-coming-off thing is quite rare.

YOUTH ALPHA

We suggest you introduce some sort of worship on week one of Youth Alpha. We tried having no form of worship. That's hard, because by the end of a ten week course, people have pretty much formed their understanding of what Christians do. They rock up to church after Alpha, you're all singing, and it becomes weird.

We tried introducing worship on the Weekend Away, and it was weird then too; people already had enough going on, being away with a bunch of strange Christians and all.

So, we recommend starting worship on the first night, because at least then everything is weird. You could start with a couple of songs led by someone on a guitar or by a band, or you could just listen to a worship song on CD.

When I lead worship for the first time on Youth Alpha, I normally say, "Hi, my name is Al, I am your worst nightmare, a Christian with a guitar." And they laugh, because it's true. Then I say, "Would you like to stand, we're going to sing together." I sing two songs and say, "Would you like to sit down?" That's it. I don't pray, start explaining stuff ("I wrote this song the day my dog died") or "coach" people in worship. John Wimber used to say, "Worship is better caught than taught" and there's a lot of truth in that. People will figure it out, and the teaching material of the course covers worship, so there's no need to add anything extra. Let them be. They probably won't sing for weeks.

WHO SHOULD LEAD WORSHIP?

On Youth Alpha, the ideal person to lead is someone of a similar age to those doing the course. They don't have to be as good as Tim Hughes, the most important thing is that they have a heart for God and can carry a tune.

WHICH SONGS SHOULD WE SING?

If you look at the fifty top songs your church sings, they will fall into two loose categories: objective songs (he is good) and subjective songs (I love you, Lord). For the first few weeks I would recommend you use objective songs. On the weekend, I would recommend that you begin to introduce some of the more subjective songs, as people are beginning to have an understanding of what a personal relationship with God looks like.

ALTERNATIVE IDEAS

People often ask us what they should do with a small Youth Alpha course, if, for example, there are only ten people having a course in someone's living room? There does come a point when it is just not practical to do sung worship, but if you can do something to reflect the values I've been talking about here, it will really help ground people in worship. Perhaps play a worship DVD or song, or have worship music playing in the background, just to introduce people to the concept of worship. See youthalpha.org for more ideas.

> *Don't worry if it feels really awkward: it feels just as awkward with hundreds of people, the only difference is that there are more people feeling awkward*

Finally, don't worry if it feels really awkward: it feels just as awkward with hundreds of people, the only difference is that there are more people feeling awkward. We've got to take the long view. This is a ten week course that may be the start of a life-long journey for those who come to faith. Worship on Youth Alpha may not seem (superficially) the most inspiring, but in many ways it is the most significant worship for our church's life. Behind the scenes, even if people look like they're having a horrible time, the Spirit of God is at work, breaking captive hearts out of jail. Bring it on!

Al Gordon is Associate Director of Worship Central and a Pastor at Holy Trinity Brompton in London.

worshipcentral.org

USING YOUTH ALPHA FOR CONFIRMATION AND IN A CATHOLIC CONTEXT

By Louisa Jacob

Youth Alpha can work very well as a pre-confirmation course, encouraging teenagers to ask questions and discover what they really think about their faith.

We have seen Youth Alpha successfully incorporated into confirmation classes across different denominations, with the specifics of confirmation being taught at the end of the course.

Youth Alpha can also work well as a post-confirmation course, encouraging those who may be wondering "what next?" to continue exploring the questions they may have.

If you are a teenager who has been through confirmation, then you may want to run Youth Alpha for others who are either thinking of being confirmed, or who are already confirmation candidates.

> *As the emphasis in Youth Alpha is on small group discussion, we have found that, after confirmation, the group will often want to continue meeting*

As the emphasis in Youth Alpha is on small group discussion, we have found that, after confirmation, the group will often want to continue meeting. Whether this is in a church or school context, it is a great opportunity to keep exploring these important issues together. Youth Alpha should always be run with a view to having a follow-up plan.

Louisa Jacob is the UK Director of Youth Alpha, and a Youth Pastor at Holy Trinity Brompton in London.

htb.org.uk

By Peter Carpentier

In a Catholic context, either during a talk or during group discussion, it is possible to reinforce Catholic teaching by referencing relevant sections from the Catholic Catechism in support of a particular topic.

Additionally, throughout the course, it is possible to emphasize the role of the Holy Spirit in Confirmation by including discussion topics rooted in Scripture and referencing the Catholic Catechism declaring the role and purpose of the gift of the Holy Spirit.

> *Provide teens with a vision of what is possible in a liturgical context*

During the Youth Alpha Weekend there is time for personal prayer for the gift of the Holy Spirit and an opportunity to attend confession. Continue this time with a liturgy designed to include youth as lectors and Eucharistic ministers. Include a contemporary worship experience led by the teens if possible. This will provide teens with a vision of what is possible in a liturgical context.

Peter Carpentier is the Founder and Director of North Shore Christian Ministries.

northshorecm.org

USING YOUTH ALPHA IN SCHOOLS

By Helen Lawson

Many teenagers today lead incredibly busy lives. They are involved in so many clubs, sports, and activities that finding time to go to another evening event may prove difficult. Running Youth Alpha in a school provides students with an opportunity to come on a lunch break, or for a short period of time after school, to ask questions and explore Christianity.

If you are a student in a school, then you are probably the best person to run a course for your friends! It is fantastic that you want to share what you believe with others. I'd encourage you to run a course with another friend or two, and make sure you have support from parents, your youth pastor, or a supportive teacher.

GET PERMISSION

If you're a student, you will probably need permission to run a course. This might be from the principal, from the chaplain (if there is one), or from another senior teacher. Most schools allow different forms of student-led lunchtime clubs, and Youth Alpha is simply another of those. Hopefully your school will be thrilled that you want to contribute to school life in this way.

If you are a youth worker, it might be a good idea to see if there are Christian contacts already involved in the school (ie: chaplain, Christian clubs, or Christian teachers) and work with them. The most effective way to work in a school is by partnering with those who are already there, and building positive relationships with them. They will be your best support network for Youth Alpha.

If there are no Christian contacts in the school, check out what other groups run at lunchtime and after school. It is important not to run Youth Alpha in competition with things that are already in place. If you are approaching a principal, have a clear picture of what you want to do,

You are probably the best person to run a course for your friends!

and be honest. Make it clear that you are coming to bless the school and to serve them as a community, not to demand entry. Also, ensure that you dress and act appropriately in accordance with teachers from the school. You need to make sure that you are aware of the school's child protection policy. Check with the leadership at the school and at your church to make sure you are covered for every eventuality.

TIME AND SPACE

So where do you start? Think about where you are going to run your group and at what time — lunchtime or after school? Ensure that you have all of the resources and materials that you need. For example, are you using multimedia that will require a DVD player/computer? Make sure you have everything on hand so that each session can run smoothly.

Think about the timing of your session. The students who come at lunchtime or after school will, no doubt, be tired from classes. You want to make the sessions fun and interactive so you can keep their attention.

Different schools will have different length breaks. It is possible to fit Youth Alpha into a thirty minute time slot — it could look something like this:

0-5 minutes: time to build relationships, eat together, relax and chat

5-15 minutes: give your talk

15-25 minutes: small group discussion time

25-30 minutes: end with some social time and invite guests back next week

Make sure that you have some social time at the beginning so students are not coming from one class to another "class." Try to make it engaging, but also try to create a relaxed space where the young people can feel comfortable and at ease.

You also need to think about the length of your course. Running the standard ten week course may not be possible within the school semester. We would recommend that you don't cut out any of the topics though, it is better to merge some together. Please remember that Youth Alpha is very flexible and can be run in eight, nine or ten weeks.

Think about who will give the talks. If you are a student, I would encourage you and your friends to do some of them. You might want to ask others from your church (if the school are happy for this to happen) or ex-pupils to come and be "guest speakers" at some sessions.

PUBLICITY

Publicizing your course is vital so that every pupil in the school knows it is happening and knows that they are invited to come. The best way to advertise is to be creative! You could promote the course with posters—make sure they look professional and fun; try to change their locations often so that they don't get stale.

Make the sessions fun and interactive so you keep their attention

You could try advertising each session individually rather than advertising the whole course at once, e.g.: "At 1 P.M. today, Fred Smith with be speaking on "Does God Heal Today?" followed by discussion and debate."

You might like to have some sort of "Launch Event" to start your course. Many schools will allow students or schools workers to speak in assembly. Maybe you could have a local Christian "celebrity" (i.e., a football player or actor) come in and and introduce Youth Alpha. Or, if assembly or celebrities are not an option, you could just have a special lunch—perhaps order a take out pizza and then do the introductory session.

YOUTH ALPHA WEEKEND/DAY AWAY

In this area in particular, every school is different. You may feel confident and able to take your group away for the weekend in order to cover the teaching material on the Holy Spirit. If you can, and the school and parents are happy, then that is great.

For those who are unable to take the group away, don't worry! There are other options. One option would be to join with another local school /church running Youth Alpha and go somewhere for a day or afternoon. If you can't get away outside of school hours, try to make these talks special in some other way. You could change your meeting from lunchtime to after school and extend it slightly, for example. Again, providing food is a good way to make it fun. One group I know ran their course each week in the school's Physics Department, but for their Holy Spirit session, they simply merged the talks together and held a special lunch in the Art Department! They didn't go far, but it made those sessions significant and different from the others.

The main thing about running Youth Alpha in a school is to have fun together. Make it engaging, build relationships, be flexible, and enjoy!

Helen Lawson is Director of Youth Alpha and Student Alpha in Scotland.

uk.alpha.org

AM I TOO YOUNG TO RUN A YOUTH ALPHA COURSE?

By Brad Hawkes

These days, the word "temple" doesn't really pop up that often, and when it does, we probably think of ancient places of worship in the Far East, or a tourist attraction we've seen on the Travel Channel. But the Bible speaks about temples over and over again. Back in the day, the temple was "the place where God lived," where people could come to get hold of Him. The temple was a big, visible reminder that God wanted to make Himself available to His people and to make sure everyone knew where to find Him.

In modern terms, you could liken the temple to a mall, a supermarket, or a fast-food joint; each of them visible with their neon signs and billboards, all claiming to have what you need to make you happy. Whether it be the golden arches with their promise of a quick burger or a Happy Meal, a Nike ad subtly suggesting that their latest high-tops are all you need to make that dunk, or another smooth iPod commercial wooing you into the world of digital downloads. All of them with something on offer. All of them visible. All of them available.

Ask any young European today if they know where they can get a fast-food fix, find a packet of cigarettes, or buy a new pair of Chuck Taylors, and they'll point you in the right direction. But try getting them to give you directions to the nearest church, or asking if they know where to find Jesus and the percentages drop. Thanks to media and technology we have pretty much everything at our fingertips, yet God appears to be less and less visible. Less and less prominent. Less and less available.

Recent surveys say that over eighty per cent of European teenagers are interested in topics regarding religion and faith. Read that again—over eighty per cent! That means young people are out looking for something, and there's more on the market to choose from than ever before. In the meantime, we Christians seem to be suffering from acute invisibility!

1 Corinthians 6:19 tells us that we are temples of the Holy Spirit. That means we are mobile, modern-day venues where God can dwell. We are living neon signs displaying God's name; walking, talking billboards making God available to our generation in our schools, universities, and workplaces. Every young person standing up for Jesus is like a 21st century temple, a point-of-contact between heaven and earth. When Sam and his Christian Union in Derby put up that poster of themselves with the words "We're all Christians, ask us why!" in their college, they turned themselves into a contact-point. When Lina from London stood up at assembly and announced that she was a Christian, or when those girls from Nottingham put up hearts with Christian messages written on them on Valentine's Day, God didn't just see a poster, a trembling girl, and red pieces of cardboard … God saw temples!

We are living neon signs displaying God's name; walking, talking billboards

So, my answer is *no,* you're not too young to run a course for your friends. By deciding to be visible in your school, college or community, you can join together with thousands of other young people across the UK, Europe, and the world, who are helping Jesus to reach a generation that He's longing to touch. You can be the point-of-contact in your world, and show your friends where to find God. You can help make God visible again in your generation.

Brad Hawkes is the National Leader of New Generation UK.

newgenerationuk.com

Igniting Young Leaders for THE Cause of Christ

By Greg Stier

Our teenagers live in a cause-centric world. Stop Global Warming! No More Bullies! Go Green! Stop Human Trafficking! Many of the causes bombarding our young leaders are good and worthy causes. But there's one cause that should rise to the top, demanding their attention, passion and action. What is this one overarching cause? It's the cause of causes – THE Cause of Christ – to make disciples who make disciples.

In Luke 19:10, Jesus describes the cause that consumed Him with these words: *"For the Son of Man came to seek and to save what was lost."* And in Matthew 28:19, He lays it out simply and succinctly when He commands His followers to *"go and make disciples."* Clearly, sharing His message with the lost is the most impacting thing His followers can be about. It's His cause. It's THE Cause of causes.

So we must help our student leaders get serious about becoming multiplying Christians who are making disciples who make disciples. We must ignite in them a passion for THE Cause of Christ and challenge them to share their faith with those God has placed in their lives. Did you know recent research shows that a friend has one hundred times more influence on another friend than a stranger does? With prayer and a little preparation, your young leaders can do more to impact their friends for Jesus than any stranger ever could. In fact, I believe God has purposefully planted them in their circle of influence so they can reach into their friends' lives with His love and His gospel message.

> *We must help our student leaders get serious about becoming multiplying Christians*

Youth Alpha provides a great opportunity for young people to step up and lead among their peers. So on a practical level, how do you help your student leaders commit to THE Cause and take seriously Jesus' call to make disciples who make disciples? Here are three key strategies that can help you ignite a passion in them to put Christ's Cause front and center in their lives.

Help your student leaders see that they are a walking, talking outreach meeting everywhere they go. Equip your leaders to do more than talk about God at Youth Alpha. Challenge them to bring God up in conversations with their friends anywhere and everywhere and show them how to move ordinary conversations toward spiritual things. For example, in a conversation where they're talking about someone's hurt feelings, they might say something like, "When I'm hurting, one of the things I do is pray . . ." Or, if they're talking with a friend about relational problems, they might say something like, "Sometimes relationships can be really tough, but the one relationship I can always count on is my relationship with God . . ." Conversation starting questions can also help your students initiate spiritual conversations. Encourage them to try thought-provoking questions like: "Do you believe there's a God?" and "If there is a God, what do you think He wants from you? . . . Would it surprise you to know He wants a relationship with you?"

Equip them to share the Gospel in a clear and compelling way. Whether it's in the midst of a youth meeting or in a casual conversation with a friend, your leaders need to know how to explain the message of the gospel. Prepare them to clearly explain the key points of Jesus' message of grace. There are a number of sound training approaches for sharing the gospel, so choose the one you like best; then train your leaders with it. At Dare 2 Share Ministries, we've found that the following GOSPEL Journey® acronym works well with teenagers.

G od created us to be with Him. (Genesis 1, 2)

O ur sins separate us from God. (Genesis 3)

S ins cannot be removed by good deeds. (Genesis 4 – Malachi 4)

P aying the price for sin, Jesus died and rose again. (Matthew – Luke)

E veryone who trusts in Him alone has eternal Life. (John)

L ife with Jesus starts now and lasts forever. (Acts – Revelation)

This acronym is not intended to be a script that's read, but rather, to provide the basic building blocks necessary for a clear and effective presentation of the message of salvation. So be sure your students understand that the key points should be woven into a conversation in a way that is relevant and meaningful for the situation at hand.

Challenge them to be relational and relentless when it comes to talking about spiritual things.
Train them to build relationships with and regularly pray for those they are seeking to influence for Jesus. Then challenge them to pursue spiritual conversations with their peers that go deeper than a superficial surface level. 2 Timothy 1:7-8 assures us: *"For God has not given us a spirit of fear and timidity, but of power, love, and self-discipline. So never be ashamed to tell others about our Lord."*
Help your young leaders learn to rely on God's power and promises as they boldly take up His cause and share His message with others and, in turn, train new believers to do the same so that the disciple-making process continues on and on in life after life.
Many teens have a hands-off attitude when it comes

> *Train them to build relationships with and regularly pray for those they are seeking to influence for Jesus*

to engaging others on a spiritual level because they see spiritual conversations as inappropriate or intrusive. But in actuality, evangelism is a search and rescue operation. It's about reaching into other's lives with Jesus' grace and truth and rescuing them from a life without hope or purpose. And it's about rescuing them from an afterlife that will be even more difficult— an eternity spent separated from God in a place the Bible describes as unbearable and unending.

Help your leaders understand that whether their peers know it or not, they need Jesus. At the core of every human is a gaping hole, a hole that can be temporarily filled with stuff, sports, or sin, to name a few of the most popular escapes. But the only thing that can truly and permanently fill that God-shaped hole is a relationship with Jesus. Life without God is like having a car without an engine or a cell phone without a service provider. It's a relationship with God that gives us hope and meaning. Teens need to understand that they can help their peers fill that invisible, unquenchable need for God by sharing the gospel with them.

But beyond the purpose and meaning that a relationship with Jesus provides in this life, student leaders must also grasp the eternal consequences. Jesus is the King of Kings and Lord of Lords who said, *"I am the way and the truth and the life. No one comes to the Father except through me"* (John 14:6). Your student leaders need to see that their peers' eternal destiny hangs in the balance.

So as you motivate and mobilize your student leaders for maximum impact in your Youth Alpha ministry, tap into the cause-centric world your teenagers inhabit and unleash them for THE Cause of causes. Teach them to continually rely on God's power and promises as they boldly take up His Cause and share His message. And then in turn, equip them to help their friends get serious about committing to THE Cause and sharing Christ with their friends as well. And on and on, until the message is multiplied out in life after life as THE Cause is lived out in our schools and communities, spreading in an unstoppable movement across this interconnected generation. With prayer and a little preparation, they can rock their world!

For free youth training and resources go to dare2share.org.

Student leaders must also grasp the eternal consequences

Greg Stier is the Founder and President of Dare 2 Share Ministries

dare2share.org

STAYING SAFE ON YOUTH ALPHA

By Rachael Heffer and Simeon Whiting
Updated for the USA by Greg and Essie Del Valle

Working with young people may well be one of the most exciting and challenging things anyone can do. Not only is it both fun and hard work at times, but it also carries a significant level of responsibility. A Youth Pastor/Leader may, at any one time, need not only to be conscious of the program, timing, and activities taking place in the venue, but also of the potential risks or hazards that there may be around them. Leaders must know how to deal with any accident or incident that may occur.

Therefore, spotting anything that could put the health and safety of a young person or a member of the team at risk is vital. For this reason, there are guidelines—and in some cases, legal requirements—which we must adhere to. For instance, if you are working with young people in Florida, there are policies in place by the Department of Children and Family Services (Social Services) that must be followed in all youth work settings. These policies help to safeguard both the young people and the youth leaders present. Wherever a youth activity is taking place, whether it's a regular event or a one-on-one, whether it's in a church, school, park or other venue, Youth Alpha group leaders will need to adhere to the policies that deal with concerns such as health and safety and child protection. Take some time to familiarize yourself with these policies, and to think about what you must do to make sure your youth work operates within them.

> *The guidelines are largely a simple matter of common sense*

Having said that, please do not be daunted by this responsibility, and do not become convinced that something is bound to go wrong! Accidents and incidents are actually very rare, so there is no need to be paranoid. All we must do is make sure that every possible precaution has been taken in order for our young people to have fun and learn in a safe environment. The guidelines that are in place to help us do this are largely a simple matter of common sense.

To help you, outlined below are nine areas that you should bear in mind as you plan your Youth Alpha course. Obviously, not all of them will apply to your situation, so just be mindful of the ones that are relevant to you.

1 RISK ASSESSMENT

It is essential to assess the risk factor of any venue you may wish to use for a youth activity, meeting, or event—regardless of where it is. Ensure you have thoroughly checked out any potential hazards and assess how problematic any highlighted areas could be. Where possible, Risk Assessment forms should be used and completed fully for your back-up and records.

Consider the likelihood of anything going wrong and ask yourself what the consequences would be should any concern turn out to be a real issue? Once these areas have been highlighted, find ways to minimize or remove the risks. If you have any doubts, make sure you seek extra advice before proceeding with your activity.

2 FIRST AID

As far as it is possible, you should have one or more people qualified in first aid and CPR on your team (make sure everyone knows who they are), and a first aid box that is easily accessible and stocked with all the basic equipment. Check that all the content— creams, etc.—are up-to-date.

Ensure that you have an easily accessible "Accident and Incident Book" where all accidents and incidents are recorded. Everything, from a cut finger to an emergency requiring a 911 call needs to be logged, written down (details included) and kept on file. This is not only to safeguard the young people, but also yourselves as youth leaders in case any complaint or query from parents (or others) is raised after an incident.

Ensure that your whole team is aware of this book and that they use it adequately—filling it in as soon as possible following any incident or accident. For training and qualifications, please visit www.redcrossonlinetraining.org.

3 FOOD HYGIENE

If you are going to be providing food on your course, think through the basics of food hygiene— talk to an expert about the essential basics you will need to take into consideration or Google Restaurant Manager Certification i.e.: www.servsafe.com. Here you'll find tons of info and quick certification classes.

Some of the vital issues include how to keep the kitchen and equipment clean and safe, how to prepare food using the right knives and chopping boards, how to store food safely and serve it at the correct temperature and making sure hot drinks are carried properly. While this may not seem like a top priority when running a Youth Alpha course, it is a key part of ensuring that your young people are kept safe and well in their environment.

4 FIRE PROCEDURES

Wherever your course takes place, the whole team should know what to do if there is a fire. This includes knowing where the fire exits are and where the assembly point is once you've left the building. Always follow fire procedures if a fire alarm goes off, even if you know it is a false alarm. If you need to leave a venue, quickly count your group to ensure that everyone is with you. Keep fire exits clear and unlocked, and keep extinguishers in their right place. Know how to use the fire alarms, how to turn them off and how to reset them. Seek advice on this before your course starts if this is unknown or unclear.

5 PARENTAL CONSENT

It is essential to obtain written permission from parents or guardians before taking young people anywhere other than your usual venue. Details of where you are going, schedules for your departure and return, what you'll be doing, etc., are all essential to include in your letter to parents. These details could be put in a letter with a tear-off slip for the parent to sign and give back to you. Do not take young people out without this permission (see Appendix 4, page 109 for a sample form, or visit alphausa. org/youthdownloads for an amendable version). You may also wish to ask parents' consent for you to make very basic decisions on behalf of their child in an emergency medical situation.

NOTE: A Medical Authorization & Release Form will allow you to expedite a decision on behalf of the parents until parents arrive at the scene or hospital. Ask parents to include their cell phone numbers in their consent forms. Download an amendable Medical Authorization & Release Form at alphausa.org/youthdownloads.

6 RELEVANT INFORMATION

When you work with young people, it is useful to have facts about each person on file so that you can easily access key information about them. Try to include information such as: full name, address, phone number, date of birth, name of parent or guardian, contact details for parent/guardian, emergency contact number, email address, any medical needs, allergies, or dietary requirements.

Keep this information secure and confidential, and do not share it with other agencies without the permission of the young person's parent or guardian. (To do so would be to disregard data protection and confidentiality guidelines of a minor.) Visit: www.hhs.gov/ocr/privacy/ for more in-depth reading.

Find ways to minimize or remove the risks

7 TRANSPORTATION

When travelling in a car or van, everyone must have a seat and seat belts must be worn—this is a legal requirement. Try and make sure an adult travels in the back of the van with the young people. Make sure your vehicle is working properly and that it is fully covered by insurance.

To adhere to *Children or Social Services Guidelines*, if you are travelling in a car please inquire from the local and/or state child agency what is the adult to student ratio per vehicle type. It's a good safety measure to pair adults together for their own safety as well as having a trustworthy witness nearby, wherever they may sit, in any vehicle larger than a car.

8 CHILD PROTECTION

Anyone who is running a Youth Alpha course should be fully trained in the basics of the Children or Social Services Guidelines. Stories of child abuse and neglect seem all too common, and sadly, the church is often seen as part of the problem, not part of the solution. This means it is essential that we act responsibly. The church, school, or other venue in which you meet should have basic Children or Social Services Guidelines which your team must follow. In the US, although this varies from state-to-state, any person working with young people or children must undergo a Personal Background Character check. For example, in Florida they must sign a, "Affidavit of Good Moral Character" form (www.dcf.state.fl.us/dcfforms/Search/DCFFormSearch. aspx) until background returns in your group's name, and have another fingerprint check through the Federal Bureau of Investigations (FBI). (This sounds intimidating, but is actually very straightforward). If you need any help with this, your organizational head office should be able to help you. Even if you know every person involved in your course really well, it is essential that everyone undergoes this procedure.

Make sure the team is clear about how to express any concerns they may have about the possible neglect or abuse of a child, and who they should talk to (See "Child Abuse Reporting Laws"). As much as possible, make sure the team knows who is with whom and what they are doing at all times—be accountable to each other. Try not to work on your own with young people but always as part of a team (even if it is with only one other leader). Never take young people out or away with fewer than two of you. If you do have to work with a young person on your own for any reason, do it in public view, making sure there are other people around, keeping the door open. Basically, be aware of how your actions look to others.

If a disclosure of some kind is made by a young person to a member of the team, ensure that the team member writes down the full details of what was shared by the young person as soon as possible after the event. You will need to have some forms accessible to you for the logging of such conversations. Encourage your team only to speak to the overall course leader about what was shared, not with other team members if there is no need. If, at any point, follow-up is required with Social Services or the police etc., written records of Who, What, Where, When and Why are valuable forms of evidence.

Don't get paranoid, but do be careful, for your own protection as well as for that of the young people you work with. These simple steps can help protect you, your young people, and your team.

Don't get paranoid, but do be careful

Child Abuse Reporting Laws - In the State of California*

Staff and volunteers are mandated reporters only while they are performing church duties. All volunteers should report any suspicion of abuse to a paid staff member immediately. From then on, it is the paid staff member who is held liable. The paid staff member must phone and write a report to a child abuse agency within 36 hours. Failure to make an abuse report is a misdemeanor punishable by up to a year in jail and/or a fine of $1,000.00. They are also subject to civil liability should the victim continue to be abused. As a mandated reporter, law for civil suits protects them unless the report is purposed to be false.

Sexual abuse is defined as sexual assault or sexual exploitation of a child.

Here are some examples to help you understand how the law is applied and the legal exceptions to the law as determined by the state legislators.

Not Reportable
1. Children fighting—where injuries are caused by children mutually fighting. (Legal exception to the reporting law)

2. Reasonable force—injuries caused by reasonable and necessary force for the purposes of self-defense, preventing the child from harming others or themselves, or to obtain possession of weapons or other dangerous objects from the child. (Legal exception to the reporting law)

3. Consensual sexual activity involving minors. If a child is 16 or 17 years old, and they have consensual sex with an adult of any age. (Legal exception to the reporting law)

4. Consensual sex between children where both children are under the age of 13. (Legal exception to the reporting law)

Reportable
1. If a child is under the age of 16 (15 years and 363 days or younger) and they have consensual sex with anyone over the age of 21.

2. If a child is 14 or 15 years old and they have consensual sex with an adult who is more than 10 years older than the child.

3. Consensual sex between two children, one under the age of 13 and the other child is 14 years old or older.

4. Any non-consensual sex of a minor.

*Laws are subject to change from year to year and vary from state to state. Please check your state website for the most current child abuse laws in your area.

9 CONFIDENTIALITY
DO promise your youth a safe place to talk, and guarantee to them that you will not gossip about what you are told, but NEVER promise complete secrecy. There may be things you need to pass on if a child's safety is at risk. If ever you feel over your head in talking to a young person, never be afraid to ask a fellow team member to assist you and join the conversation.

Hopefully the issues noted in this article will provide some basic guidelines for you to think about when you are planning your Youth Alpha course. In all things, remember that while it brings great responsibility, it is also a privilege to work with young people and to see God so at work in their lives.

Greg and Essie Del Valle are the Executive Directors of Lakeland Teen Challenge International Inc.

teenchallengegirls.com,
newlifeacademyinternational.com
and teenchallengeusa.com

Simeon Whiting and Rachael Heffer work for British Youth for Christ.

yfc.co.uk

YOUTH MINISTRY 3.0 – A MANIFESTO OF CHANGE

By Mark Oestreicher

There's a series of commercials on American TV for a hamburger chain. The commercials show ordinary people—often guys—wearing the long red braids of the chain's logo character, and having countercultural epiphanies about burgers and other fast-food realities. My favorite of these commercials opens with an aerial shot of a massive hole in the ground, and hundreds of people are running toward it from all sides. When they get to the hole, they all jump in.

Then the shot changes to catch the face of one guy (wearing the red wig) who's running amid the crowd. As he's running, we can hear his thoughts as he realizes that something isn't right. He then starts to speak as it dawns on him that he doesn't have to have his burgers cooked ahead of time and kept warm under a heat lamp. He slows to a stop, and a few others also stop to listen—but most of the crowd continue to run into the hole. The few who stop with him all decide that they want their burgers to sizzle! They cheer and start running back—against the flow of the crowd.

It's a funny commercial. But I have to admit that every time I see it, it reminds me of the church. We have all this momentum. We perceive things are going well. Our megachurches are more mega than ever. Our youth ministries are better funded than ever. Youth ministry is receiving more respect than ever. We have better resources and training events and celebrities and credibility than we've ever had.

So why does it seem like we're racing into a hole?

I want to be part of that countercultural band of youth workers who stop. I want to be part of that "wait a second" group who doesn't just accept the way things are. I want to join with others who notice that we're heading down a path toward obsolescence and complete ineffectiveness, and turn around to ask, "What should we change?"

I believe we're at a crossroad in youth work. In order to be effective—in order to be true to our calling—we need to change. We need to turn at this crossroad, but I'm afraid we're passing right through it, assuming that the way we've always done things will continue to work.

The problem is this: the way we're doing things is already not working. We're failing at our calling, and deep down, most of us know it. This is why we need an epochal shift in our assumptions, approaches, models, and methods.

It's time for Youth Ministry 3.0.

AN EXTREMELY SHORT HISTORY

Adolescence is a cultural phenomenon, and it's fairly recent. It's only in the last 100 years or so that our Western cultures have acknowledged a period of time between childhood and adulthood. And youth culture itself is even more recent—it's really only about sixty years old.

Sure, this is a generalization, but it's not unfair to break modern youth culture into three epochs. We could say that the first epoch was post World War II until about 1970 (I've started calling this "Youth Culture 1.0"). The second epoch was roughly between 1970 and the turn of the millennium ("Youth Culture 2.0"). And we're living in the third epoch now ("Youth Culture 3.0").

> *I believe we're at a crossroad in youth work*

THE THREE TASKS OF ADOLESCENCE

All teenagers, at least those who live in a culture that acknowledges adolescence, wrestle with three "tasks": identity, autonomy, and affinity. I refer to them as tasks, though they're wrestled with almost completely semiconsciously. The older a teenager gets, the more self-aware they become of this wrestling, of these tasks (and certainly more so these days since adolescence now stretches into the twenties). But the tasks present themselves at the onset of adolescence.

Identity is the, "Who am I?" question. Simply put: one's identity is the sum of one's self-perceptions. This includes self-perceptions about character, values, purpose, and potential in life; caste; emotional makeup; appearance and body type; intellectual, spiritual, and emotional strength or weakness; relationship to family, friends, and culture at large as well as many other factors.

Children and pre-teens aren't intellectually capable of this kind of third-person thought. A nine-year-old cannot stand apart from herself and perceive herself—she cannot form opinions of herself based on self-perception. She can form opinions about herself based only on what she likes or doesn't like, and what others have said about her.

This is why identity is such a major task in adolescence. The reality is that by the time an adolescent reaches her mid-twenties, her identity will be mostly formed. (And, remember, this is the whole point of culture giving teenagers a respite between childhood and adulthood.) Sure, we continue to shape and refine our identities throughout adulthood, but the core formation work is done. The course is mostly set.

Autonomy simply refers to something's separateness—it's independence. In adolescent-development terms, autonomy is wrestling with the questions, "How am I unique and different?" and, "What's my unique contribution?"

In psychological terms, this is often referred to as *individuation*. The process of individuation is becoming oneself: unique, and separate. This process is primarily (though not exclusively) the issue of separating from one's family.

Mixed into this progression is the ancillary question, "What's my unique contribution?" The "contribution" in that question plays out in a variety of arenas: family, friends, and other relationships; school; youth group; community and the world. As a teenager begins to see her uniqueness, she's better equipped to understand her role and influence in relationships and the world around her. As she begins to see how that influence plays out, she's better equipped to grasp her uniqueness.

Affinity, as a word, simply means likeness or attraction. We use it in a developmental sense to refer to people's connection to others who are like them in some way. This "likeness" may be external —a teenage boy may find affinity with guys who are into skateboarding or science, or a teenage girl may find affinity with a group of kids who like a certain style of music. But the likeness can also be more internal. A teenager can find affinity with others who share the same values or the same outlook on life, or he can find affinity with his family based on shared experiences and stories.

This final task of adolescence almost seems in opposition to the task of autonomy. But, in reality, they go hand in hand—two apparent opposites in a dependent dance, with identity looking on. Autonomy and affinity are the yin and yang of identity formation, really, informing and framing that first task.

It's easy to see this quest for affinity in teenagers. They desperately desire to be included, to be part of a social network, to feel as though they belong somewhere. Young and middle teens, especially, commonly have multiple affinity groups to which they belong (or aspire to belong). This is all a normal (sometimes healthy, sometimes not) part of the process of figuring out who they are.

SHIFTING PRIORITIES

I believe (and I'm finding good support for this idea from those more academic than me!) that these three adolescent tasks have remained constant, but their prioritization has shifted over the three epochs of youth culture. In Youth Culture 1.0, "the long leg of the three-legged stool" (as I've started to call it) was identity. Youth culture was new, and was trying to figure out who it was. It was still very much a sub-culture of culture at large, and not dramatically influential to the world of adults.

Ever since caring adults started trying to connect with teenagers, youth work, has been cross-cultural, missional work. In many ways, the earliest modern youth workers (during those post World War II days, when Youth Culture 1.0 was just getting some traction) were motivated almost purely by missionary zeal. They wanted to bring the love of Christ to a different cultural grouping of people, and thought long and hard about how to embody the gospel in ways that were culturally appropriate. We could say that Youth Ministry 1.0 was proclamation-driven, and had key values of *evangelism* and *correction*.

But in the late 1960s, as youth culture came into its own, and was clearly no longer a passing cultural fad, the priorities of the three adolescent tasks went through a shift. Youth Culture 1.0 was already "other" and "different," which gave it a natural sense of autonomy. But as youth culture became more accepted and normative, the adolescent need for autonomy exerted itself and became the leading task. Identity and affinity started to be worked out *in the context* of autonomy.

Youth work also went through a dramatic shift as youth workers, trying to be true to their calling, shifted their assumptions, approaches, and methods to reach teenagers. Youth workers responded (appropriately, it's important to remember) with new tools to build autonomous youth groups. Youth Ministry 2.0 became *program*-driven, with key values of *discipleship* and *building a positive peer group*.

> *Youth Ministry 1.0 was* proclamation-*driven, and had key values of* evangelism *and* correction

But a third shift in youth culture has taken place. We might say that Youth Culture 2.0 was so successful in its quest for autonomy that it left a "belonging vacuum." As youth culture became the dominant culture in our society (with adult culture now looking to youth for cues in almost every arena), youth culture responded by splintering. We now find ourselves in a time when there is no longer one monolithic youth culture. There are now multiple youth cultures, each with its own values, behaviors, attitudes, styles, music, language, and relational norms.

Youth Culture 3.0 is defined by a priority of affinity, the need to belong. For today's teenagers, identity and autonomy are worked out *in the context* of the quest for affinity.

AND HERE'S THE RUB

Many of us have sensed that something is wrong with how we're doing youth work. We've been like those people in the commercial, running towards the big whole in the ground, utilizing our finely tuned programs in an attempt to reach teenagers who just don't give a rip about our games, entertainment, and well-crafted youth sermons, but thinking there must be a different way of living out our calling.

We see the current dropout rates of teenagers after youth ministry, and we think (with our Youth Ministry 2.0 mindsets): "We need to add cooler programs! We need a big youth center—on the other side of the parking lot from the church! We need better games! We need a state-of-the-art sound system!"

We see kids in our ministries with shallow, unarticulated faith, and we think, "We need a better curriculum! We need more mission trips to shock them! We need a small groups program—let's see how HTB or Soul Survivor does it! We need to increase the youth budget so we can do better stuff!"

Alas, our thinking is stuck in—let's face it—the previous millennium. We *cannot* build a great youth ministry to reach Youth Culture 3.0 teenagers with Youth Ministry 2.0 methods or thinking.

YOUTH MINISTRY 3.0

Instead of the evangelism and correction themes of Youth Ministry 1.0 or the discipleship and create-a-positive-peer-group themes of Youth Ministry 2.0, we need to embrace the key themes of *communion* and *mission*.

COMMUNION

For teenagers desperate to define their identities through affinity, we need to help them experience true community. True community doesn't mean once-a-week, highly programed youth group meetings. True community *might* take place in the context of a small group— but the practice and programing of small groups does not ensure true community. True community is life-on-life, whole life, eating together, sharing journeys, working through difficulties, wrestling with praxis (theology in practice), accountability, safety, openness, serving side-by-side, cultivating shared passion and holy discontent, mutuality, and a host of other variables. True community *is not* a program. It's not something people sign up for. It's not something we force.

> *Youth Ministry 2.0 became* program-driven, with key values of discipleship *and* building a positive peer group

But "community" doesn't seem to completely capture Youth Ministry 3.0 thematically. Instead, let's make the subtle but significant shift to the value of *communion*. Communion is true community with Christ in the mix. Communion is both the *essence* and the *action* of a Christ community.

MISSION

"Mission" and "missional" have become buzzwords over the past few years. I'm concerned they're becoming faddish, which would be a great loss as they're so massively pregnant with truth, value, and scriptural integrity. For our purposes here, let's describe "missional" as "joining up with the mission of God in the world."

Mission, in this context, is *not* about having a purpose or mission statement. It's not about being purposeful (although that's not a bad thing) or purpose-driven. And I'm *definitely* not using the word "mission" to describe starting a program of missions. Mission, in this context, starts with the assumption that God is already actively working on earth, bringing redemption, restoration, and the transformation of all creation. Therefore, a missional ministry seeks to discern, observe, and identify what's close to the heart of God and where God is already at work— and then *joins up with the work of God already in progress.*

Combine these two themes—communion and mission—and you have a youth ministry that could be described as communion on a mission: a Christ-infused, true community seeking to engage the world in God's redemptive work-in-progress. Can you see how this provides meaning and direction to all three adolescent tasks?

"My identity is a follower of Jesus Christ, framed in real community with others who have a synergistic, shared passion for the work of God in the world."

"My uniqueness (autonomy) is found both in the individuality of my own story, as well as in the unique ways in which my contextualized community seeks to live out faith in Christ, together and for others."

"My affinity is with these people, for these people, with Christ, and for the active work of God in the world."

Whereas Youth Ministry 1.0 was proclamation-driven and Youth Ministry 2.0 was program-driven, Youth Ministry 3.0 needs to be … not-driven. It's time to do away with being driven or driving. That metaphoric language might work for herds of cattle, but it doesn't work for a fluid, missional community.

Instead, let's say *present*. Present to the work of God in our lives and in the world. Present to the moment, not just living for a day when we leave a horrible world. Present to one another—to those experiencing communion with us, to those who aren't (yet), and even to those who never will be in our community. Present to life in the way of Jesus.

> *Youth Ministry 3.0 needs to be … not-driven. It's time to do away with being driven or driving*

Figuring out what all of this looks like in real youth work is going to take lots of experimentation and failure. We'll need to be passionate about contextualization and not just copy each other. Let's remember these fantastic words that Jesus said as He was sending out the disciples: "Don't think you have to put on a fundraising campaign before you start. You don't need a lot of equipment. *You are the equipment*, and all you need to keep that going is three meals a day. Travel light" Matthew 10:9-10 (*The Message*, emphasis mine).

Mark Oestreicher is the former president of Youth Specialties. This article is based on Mark's book, *Youth Ministry 3.0* (Zondervan/Youth Specialties, 2009).

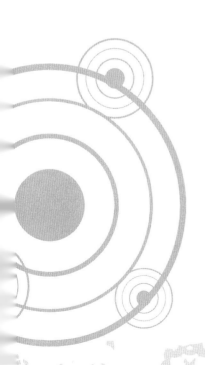

SECTION 3

YOUTH ALPHA TEAM TRAINING

TEAM TRAINING SESSION 1

HOW TO LEAD SMALL GROUPS ON YOUTH ALPHA

TEAM TRAINING SESSION 1
HOW TO LEAD SMALL GROUPS ON YOUTH ALPHA

SUMMARY

AIMS OF THIS SESSION

- To equip team members to run a fantastic Youth Alpha course

- To explain how small groups work

- To empower team members to lead small groups confidently

NOTES

- We strongly recommend that every Youth Alpha course includes the following team training session. Why not get together one evening, have a meal, work through this training material and pray for your course together?

- This session should be held before the course begins

SESSION OVERVIEW

- Food
- Welcome
- Worship
- Talk
    - Introduction
    - Point 1 – Youth Alpha course overview
    - Point 2 – Aims of the small group
    - Point 3 – Practicalities of small groups
    - Point 4 – Tips for leaders
    - Point 5 – Ground rules for your small group
    - Point 6 – Praying in your small group
    - Conclusion
- Group activity – Small group role-play

INTRODUCTION

- Welcome to the Youth Alpha course team training! It's great to have you as part of our team!

- The aim of this session is to give you an idea of what will happen on the course and to equip you to be able to lead a Youth Alpha small group

If your team don't know each other very well, you may wish to start with an ice breaker game to help them start to learn some names.

POINT 1 – YOUTH ALPHA COURSE OVERVIEW

1. WHY ARE WE RUNNING THIS COURSE?

- Some of you may have lots of experience with Youth Alpha, others will have done a course, and some won't know anything

- So let me quickly tell you why we're running the course

- The aim is to give our friends a chance to hear more about what we, as Christians, believe, and to give them a chance to experience what being a part of a Christian community is like. Our hope is that as they hear about Jesus and discuss what they think, they will find that it is true and they may want to set off on a journey of faith with God

- Here's what this course is not:

  - a place where we only want certain opinions voiced

  - a chance to "Bible-bash" our friends

  - a place to pressure people into making a decision for Jesus

  - a guaranteed way to "convert" people

- Youth Alpha is a tool we can use to offer our friends a chance to explore the Christian faith and learn about the person of Jesus Christ

2. HOW DOES THE COURSE WORK?

- The course runs over eight/nine/ten sessions/weeks *[delete as appropriate]*

- Each session will have the following elements:

Food

- We'll start each session by eating together. *[Explain the context of this—whether it will be a meal, snacks, or another option you have chosen]*

- We believe that there is something spiritual about eating together—Jesus did a lot of His ministry around meals. It's a great way to build community, too

Fun

- The aim is for every session to be fun. This course is not meant to be heavy or intense. If you have any ideas on how we can make it more fun, please share them

- We might play a game or show a funny video to start the session. We believe that you can learn about Jesus and have fun at the same time!

Talk

- Each session, one of us will give a talk

- That's our chance, as a team, to say what we want to about Christianity—and it's our *only* chance. If it isn't said in the talk, it doesn't need to be said at all

- Each talk will be on one of the suggested Youth Alpha topics

- The idea is that the talks should be appealing and relevant to the group. We will use illustrations and different media to make it interesting

Small groups

- Every Youth Alpha session has small group discussion time. This is the most important part of the whole course, and it's vital that we get this right

- That's really why we're doing this training session—so we are all equipped and ready to host and lead the small groups

- So those are the four components of the course

- There's also a Youth Alpha Weekend/Day in the middle of the course which you should already have on your calendar. We'll talk more about that in a few weeks at our next training session

- For the rest of this session, we're going to look at how Youth Alpha small groups work and how we can lead them well

POINT 2 – AIMS OF THE SMALL GROUP

- Let's start by having a look at how a small group might work

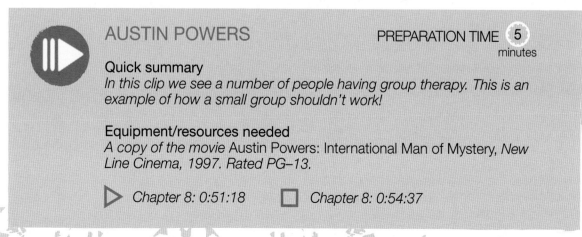

AUSTIN POWERS

PREPARATION TIME ⑤ minutes

Quick summary
In this clip we see a number of people having group therapy. This is an example of how a small group shouldn't work!

Equipment/resources needed
A copy of the movie Austin Powers: International Man of Mystery, *New Line Cinema, 1997. Rated PG–13.*

▷ *Chapter 8: 0:51:18* ☐ *Chapter 8: 0:54:37*

Projector and screen (or a TV), and a DVD player.

How to link to talk
- That's an example of how your small group shouldn't work! A Youth Alpha small group has quite a different feel—it is not like a self-help group. No matter how annoying the people in your group may be, it's a good thing to *not* want to kill them!

- So why do we have small groups?

- Jesus had small groups! He had a group of twelve guys that He hung out with, and they certainly asked lots of questions (in a way, you could say the disciples were the first Youth Alpha small group!)

- There are two main aims of small groups—to discuss, and to build relationships

1. TO DISCUSS

- The British band Coldplay wrote a song called "Square One" which goes like this:

  "You're in control, is there anywhere you wanna go?
  You're in control, is there anything you wanna know?
  The future's for discovering
  The space in which we're travelling
  From the top of the first page
  To the end of the last day
  From the start in your own way
  You just want somebody listening to what you say
  It doesn't matter who you are."

- This pretty much sums up the way a lot of people think these days. On one hand, we are in control of our own lives, but on the other hand, we really just want someone to listen to our thoughts

- Youth Alpha gives people the chance to express their views on life and faith. The best way to do this is through discussion

- This is very important—we want people to be able to say what they really think

- Youth Alpha is about helping people to make the right decisions, rather than just telling them the right answers. We don't just want them to know the facts, we want them to be able to figure stuff out and find the answers for themselves

- If we allow this to happen, then the fruit will be long-lasting, rather than short-term

- Discussion helps truth to rise to the surface, making it easier for people to discover it for themselves

- In John 16:13, it says, "But when he, the Spirit of truth, comes, he will guide you into all truth.

He will not speak on his own; he will speak only what he hears, and he will tell you what is yet to come"

- We don't need to be afraid of people's questions. As that verse says, the Spirit will lead us into truth—and if something is true, it will stand up against any amount of questioning

- We have one golden rule in small groups—**no question is too simple or too hostile**

- We need to make it easy for people to discuss whatever they like, including questions about faith and Christianity, or issues that the course material might have raised for them

2. TO BUILD RELATIONSHIPS

- Someone once said that people go to church for many reasons, but only come back for one—if they make friends

- Hopefully the people in your small group will really enjoy hanging out and getting to know each other better

- This aspect of the Youth Alpha course is so important; it's essential to spend time getting to know each other and letting friendships form

POINT 3 – PRACTICALITIES OF SMALL GROUPS

1. WHEN ARE THE SMALL GROUPS?

If you are aiming to have small groups after the talk:

- After the talk, we will split into our groups and go to different parts of the venue for our discussion time. *[It might be good to have more drinks and cookies available for this]*

- Wherever you are situated, you must make sure that everyone in the group feels comfortable and safe. We need to ensure that everyone sits on the same level—either on chairs, sofas or the floor, but not a combination of these, as it will make the group dynamic feel odd

- It is vital that all small groups finish on time, if not early. It is better to leave people wanting more than letting them get bored—you can always continue the discussion next time. Be ruthless about sticking to your finish time—even if someone is making the best point ever!

- Finishing on time offers people security, especially if they're feeling unsure about being on the course in the first place. There's nothing worse than people not coming back because the group went on so late the first week

- Do use the suggested questions in the *Leaders' Guide* as a starter for your small group discussion, but feel free to talk about whatever you'd like

If you are planning to have small groups within the talk, after each teaching point:

- The person giving the talk will tell you how long you have for each block of discussion —probably no more than five or ten minutes. Small groups will stay in the main room for discussion, otherwise too much time will be spent going to and from groups

- Do use the suggested questions in the *Leaders' Guide* as a starter for your small group discussion, but feel free to talk about whatever you'd like

2. WHO IS IN THE GROUP?

- Small groups usually have between eight and twelve members, but there should never be more than twelve people in a group

- Ideally, each group should have one or two "leaders" and one or two "helpers"

- The leaders are there to guide the discussion and host the group. Normally, leaders are Christians who have done the course before

- The helpers are there to help host the group and to make guests feel welcome. They may help get drinks and food for people, make introductions, and generally be encouraging and helpful

- There should be between six and eight guests per group—people who are there to do the course but aren't on the team

- If you are a helper, there is one really important thing to remember: **you should not talk** in the group discussion unless the leader specifically asks you to. You're there as a silent prayer support to the leader—it may well be that some of the guests don't even realize until halfway through the course that you are on the team, which is fine!

3. HOW DO WE START THE GROUP ON THE FIRST NIGHT?

- On the first night when you get into your small group for the first time, I'd suggest you start with some sort of group ice breaker game. This may seem really uncomfortable but it is worth doing

- The important thing is to learn each person's name in a way that helps everyone else remember it

- Suggestions include *[please feel free to suggest your own]*:

1. **The name game:** starting with the group leader, each person must say their first name preceded by a word that starts with the same letter. The word must describe their personality, for example: Macho Matt, Super Sarah, Phunny Phil, etc. The next person must start by saying the name(s) of those before them, and then say their own, so that the last person has lots of names to remember!

2. **Favorites:** each person must say their name, and then tell the group what their favorite film/book/TV program/song is

3. **The elevator game:** each person must say their name, followed the name of the person

they'd most like to be stuck in an elevator with (this person could be famous, dead, alive … there are no restrictions)

4. **The desert island game:** each person must say their name, and then tell the group what one luxury item they'd take with them if they were stranded on a desert island

- It can also be a good idea to ask why each person has come to Youth Alpha. If you know anything about your group beforehand (maybe through chatting while you eat) then start by asking someone whom you know will give a negative response

- This will allow everyone else to be as honest as they like. If the first person says, "I just want to know Jesus better," chances are that everyone else will feel too embarrassed to say what they really think. What you want is someone who can say, "I'm only here because my friend dragged me. I would rather be anywhere else in the world than here. I'm an atheist and this is all a load of rubbish." That would be perfect!

POINT 4 – TIPS FOR LEADERS

1. WE'RE THERE TO FACILITATE DISCUSSION

- Remember that the role of the small group is not so much to answer people's questions as it is to facilitate discussion

- The best phrase you can use is, "What do the rest of you think . . .?"

- So when someone offers a thought, it's not your job to jump in with your views or an answer, but to throw it open to the rest of the group. Let me demonstrate what I mean

BALL SKETCH

PREPARATION TIME 0
minutes

Quick summary
In this illustration, you (and six or seven volunteers) will demonstrate the "perfect" Alpha small group discussion time.

Equipment / resources needed
Enough chairs for six or seven people
A ball

How it works
Ask for six or seven volunteers (this could be all of your team, which would be great).
Get them to sit in a semi-circle facing the rest of the group (you can either ask them to bring a chair, or have some already set up). Get hold of a ball. Then explain:

- *These six/seven people represent a Youth Alpha small group, and we are going to demonstrate how an ideal discussion should work. I am the small group leader*

- Normally a group would sit in a circle—just so you know

- We're going to demonstrate visually how a discussion works, so let's pretend that whoever has the ball is the person who is speaking

- There are three ways a small group *could* work:

MODEL 1 – WRONG

- So I have the ball, and I would start off by saying something like, "What did everyone think of the talk tonight?" Someone would hopefully answer that *[throw someone the ball—they don't actually have to answer. Ask that person to throw it back to you—then throw it to them, and ask them to throw it back to you—keep doing this]*

- Now you can see that if the small group works like this, then there are two of us having a great discussion—but the rest of the group are bored

- This is how NOT to do your small group on Youth Alpha!

MODEL 2 – WRONG

- Another way of running your small group is like this *[quietly tell your group to always throw the ball back to you]*:

- I can start off the conversation by asking *[insert name]* a question. S/he passes it back to me, so I pass it on to *[insert name of someone else]*. S/he passes it back to me *[keep this going]*

- Although the whole group is involved in the conversation, it's still all about me, the leader. This is also NOT how the ideal small group works

MODEL 3 – RIGHT

- Here's how the ideal small group goes *[quietly tell your group to pass the ball among themselves, occasionally returning to you]*:

- Again, I start off the discussion, but this time the group chats among themselves

- Occasionally it may return to me, but I simply ask another question or say, "What do others think?" to keep the conversation focused on the group.

- This is the perfect small group discussion! The conversation is flowing and everyone is contributing by saying what they really think

How to link to talk
Ask for a round of applause for your volunteers, thank them, and ask them to return to their seats.

- So, a small group leader is more of a facilitator than an instructional guru. A facilitator is simply another member of the group who is helping to keep the discussion going. Our views are no more important than anyone else's, and we are not looking to judge people or their opinions. It is our aim to guide and steer the group, so ask lots of questions!

- Remember the key question for leaders: "And what do the rest of you think?"

2. THEY'VE ALREADY HAD THE TALK

- This is a key point to grasp. Remember that by the time we're ready for our small group discussion, everyone has already heard a talk; they certainly don't want to hear another one. Preaching of any kind is banned in the group

- This can be hard, especially if people are asking questions that you consider easy to answer—but don't do it

- You might be leading a group who seem to have disproved every aspect of Christianity. Even so, don't try and defend it

- You might get asked lots of questions and want to answer them—don't! Far better to say something like, "That's a great question—what do the rest of you think?"

- By session six (or so) of the course, your group may want to know what you think about certain subjects, and only then might it be appropriate to share. We need to earn our right to talk by listening for the first half of the course

3. LOOK FOR OPINIONS NOT ANSWERS

- Avoid asking closed questions—questions that have either "yes" or "no" as an answer. Instead, ask open-ended questions that require an opinion

- This helps to keep the discussion flowing, but it also means that there can be no right or wrong answer; you are asking for an opinion and because we respect each person, no one can be incorrect

- Ask what people *think* or *feel* in order to keep things open

4. VALUE EVERY OPINION

- Don't take sides in the discussion, but value every opinion that is shared

- Even if someone says something that seems crazy or ridiculous—we want them to know that what they think matters to the group

- You could say something like, "That's interesting. What does everybody else think?" This allows you to affirm them without having to agree, and it gives others in the group a chance to respond for themselves

5. DON'T BE AFRAID TO LOSE THE ARGUMENT!

- This is also really important. If you get to the end of the night and your small group have, say,

disproved the resurrection, don't worry! Actually—this is great! You may be discouraged, but the chances are that your group will come back next week in order to disprove the next topic. Just remember—if truth is truth, it will always come out

- This is a really hard thing to do, and takes discipline on your part as leader

You may wish to include the following optional extra, but it is not essential

---

OPTIONAL EXTRA – GOING DEEPER

"FEELING DISCOURAGED" TESTIMONY

If you have a story about a time when you were feeling discouraged by a small group discussion, regardless of whether everything worked out or whether you felt that you failed, then share it now. It will encourage those who are nervous about getting it wrong.

POINT 5 – GROUND RULES FOR YOUR SMALL GROUP

- Youth Alpha is not supposed to be like school (at all!) but it might be helpful to set some ground rules, as a group, on the first week. These could include things like:

1. NO PUT-DOWNS

- We want everyone to respect each other. It's okay for the group to attack ideas, but not each other

2. THERE'S NO SUCH THING AS A STUPID QUESTION

- We want everyone to know it's okay to ask *any* question without being laughed at

3. NO ONE HAS TO TALK BUT ONLY ONE PERSON TALKS AT A TIME

- We won't make anyone speak

- We want to respect each other, and that means listening to what others have to say and not talking over them

4. WHAT IS SAID IN THE GROUP STAYS IN THE GROUP

- If someone shares something personal in the group, there needs to be an understanding that it will not be passed on to others at school or anywhere else. The exception is if something is shared that is harmful to the person, this legally needs to be reported to authorities

POINT 6 – PRAYING IN YOUR SMALL GROUP

- One of the goals of the small group is to model praying together

- It is always good to remember not to rush into prayer, though. Go at the pace of the slowest person in your group—if they are not ready, don't do it

- There's nothing worse than trying to have a time of prayer that goes a bit like this:

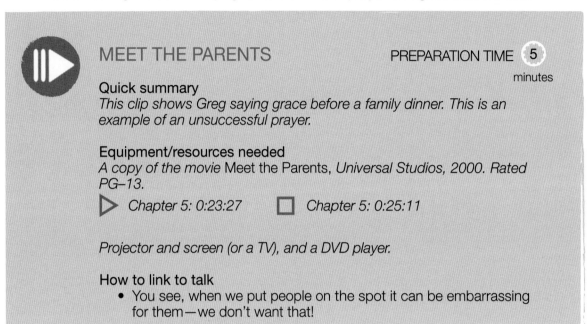

MEET THE PARENTS

PREPARATION TIME **5** minutes

Quick summary
This clip shows Greg saying grace before a family dinner. This is an example of an unsuccessful prayer.

Equipment/resources needed
A copy of the movie Meet the Parents, *Universal Studios, 2000. Rated PG–13.*

▷ *Chapter 5: 0:23:27*   ☐ *Chapter 5: 0:25:11*

Projector and screen (or a TV), and a DVD player.

How to link to talk
- You see, when we put people on the spot it can be embarrassing for them—we don't want that!

- There may be people in the group for whom Youth Alpha is their first experience of anything church-related; they may not be comfortable praying with everyone else until later in the course

- The earliest we would suggest you try praying together is after the talk "Why and how do I pray?"—Session 4

- If you do decide to have a time of prayer, the leader should test the waters by suggesting that it might be cool if the group prayed together

- Make it clear that no one has to pray aloud, but they're all welcome to. We suggest that the small group leader prays a very short and simple prayer first, something like, "Thank you, God, for the weather. Amen."

- If you are in your small group and you feel a long and eloquent prayer coming on, do pray it, but not until you get home!

- If the leader prays the world's most powerful and beautiful prayer, chances are the group will think, "Wow, if that's what prayer is, I could never do that." If we pray a simple prayer, however, the group may think, "Hey, that was simple. I could do way better than that," and they probably will!

CONCLUSION

- To conclude, small groups are an absolutely key part of the course

- If we get them right, they will be the most enjoyable part too, and our groups will love being together

- Remember:

    - it's a discussion, not a question and answer session

    - no preaching

    - value all people and their opinions

    - finish on time, no matter what

- In a minute we're going to practice being part of a small group

- Before we do that, let's look at one final video—about how *not to* lead an Alpha small group

HOW NOT TO RUN A SMALL GROUP

PREPARATION TIME 5 minutes

Quick summary
This clip shows a "computer simulation" of how to run a small group—or not. (This film stars Jamie Haith, head of Student Alpha, who does all the voices, too.)

Equipment/resources needed
To find the link for this clip, please visit youthalpha.org/lgmedia
You may want to use a projector and a screen in order to show the clip to the whole group.

How to link to talk
- So that's how not to do it!

GROUP ACTIVITY

SMALL GROUP ROLE-PLAY

PREPARATION TIME 15 minutes

Quick summary
A small group role-play demonstrating how, and how not, to lead a group.

Equipment/resources needed
One envelope per group.
Eight cue cards to go inside each envelope. You can find the cue cards on Sheet 10 at the end of this session, or online at www.alphausa.org/ youthdownloads

How it works

Get people into groups of eight (there are eight cue cards in each envelope).

Each person must take a cue card at random from the envelope—this will tell them which "character" they are to be.

Tell the groups:

- In each group there is one helper and one leader—please identify yourself if this is you

- No one else should identify themselves—it's more fun that way

- "Guests," I want you to pretend that it is the first week of Youth Alpha, and that you have just listened to the talk "Who Is Jesus?"

- "Leaders," the first thing you need to do is introduce everyone, and play some sort of ice breaker game (maybe the "name game"?)

- Leaders, you should ask each of your group why they have come—and the rest of you must make up a reason that fits your character

- Then, start to discuss the talk, and you *must* stick to the role you have been given

- We will give you thirty minutes *[or set another time limit]* to do both the welcome game and the discussion—then we'll hear some feedback about how you got on

CLOSE OF SESSION

Once everyone is finished, get feedback from groups (maybe ask one or two people from each group to speak for their "team")

- How did you get along?

- What was difficult about that?

- What was easy about that?

- Which character was the hardest to handle?

- In what way is leading a Youth Alpha group different from leading other types of groups *[if relevant]*?

You might like to close in prayer, praying for the team and the course.

This training session is based on the article "How to lead a Youth Alpha small group" by Matt Costley. To read the article in full please see page 42.

SHEET 10
CUE CARDS —
SMALL GROUP ROLE-PLAY

youthalpha.

Print as many copies of this sheet as you think you will need, depending on the number of groups. Insert one copy of each character into each group's envelope, ensuring there are only eight roles in total.

THE LEADER
You are the leader of this group. Your role is to facilitate the discussion, and make sure that everyone has an opportunity to speak. Don't let anyone dominate the discussion, and remember to follow the guidelines you were given earlier.

THE HELPER
You are the helper. You many not speak unless the leader asks you to.

THE ATHEIST
You don't believe in God, or in any "higher power." You think anyone who believes in such things must be crazy and illogical. Argue this point in a non-hostile way.

THE THINKER
Your big question (which you should come back to often) is, "If there is a God, why is there so much suffering in the world?"

THE OVERLY-SINCERE CHRISTIAN
You are a super-keen Christian and cannot believe that anyone could doubt there is a God. You know your Bible backwards and you should quote Bible verses to the group as often as you can get away with.

THE TALKER
You are going to be loud and slightly obnoxious—you don't think you believe in God, but aren't really sure. However, you love to hear the sound of your own voice and should try to speak as often as you can, over the top of others if need be.

THE QUIET ONE
You are quiet and you don't like to say *anything*, even if asked. You should refuse to answer questions—just sit there and look awkward.

THE SEEKER
You are genuinely interested in discussing this theme, and want to know what others think. You will support the leader if any disputes arise, and you just want to be able to have a good, interesting discussion.

TEAM TRAINING SESSION 2

HOW TO PRAY FOR EACH OTHER ON YOUTH ALPHA

TEAM TRAINING SESSION 2
HOW TO PRAY FOR EACH OTHER ON YOUTH ALPHA

SUMMARY

AIMS OF THIS SESSION

- To equip team members to run a fantastic Youth Alpha Weekend/Day

- To explain how the weekend/day prayer ministry time works

- To empower team members to pray for each other and their groups

NOTES

- We strongly recommend that every Youth Alpha course includes the following team training session. Why not get together one evening, have a meal, work through this training material and pray for your course together?

- This session should be held a week or two before the Youth Alpha Weekend/Day

SESSION OVERVIEW
- Food
- Welcome
- Worship
- Talk
    - Introduction
    - Point 1 – Youth Alpha Weekend/Day overview
    - Point 2 – What is prayer ministry?
    - Point 3 – Four values of prayer ministry
    - Point 4 – Practical tips
    - Conclusion
- Group activity – Prayer ministry time

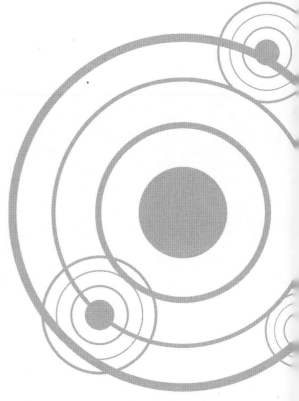

INTRODUCTION

- Welcome to the second Youth Alpha team training session!

- The aim of this session is to give you an idea of what will happen on the Youth Alpha Weekend/Day and to equip you to be able to pray for the people in your Youth Alpha small group

If your team doesn't know each other very well, you may wish to start with an ice breaker game to help them start to learn some names.

POINT 1 – YOUTH ALPHA WEEKEND/DAY OVERVIEW

1. WHY DO WE HAVE A WEEKEND/DAY?

- The weekend is the only part of the course that includes teaching on the person and work of the Holy Spirit

- It also gives us the chance to pray for our groups to be filled with the Holy Spirit. It's a chance for them to experience the love of God

- It is often the most fun bit and I think you'll find that the relationships in your group become much stronger as a result of the Weekend/Day *[delete as applicable]*

2. HOW DOES THE WEEKEND/DAY WORK?

- We're going to be holding the Weekend/Day at *[venue]* from *[date/time]* to *[date/time]*

- We're getting there by *[insert mode of transportation]*

- And here's how the program will work:

[Describe the program for the your weekend/day—see the sample programs in Appendix 3 (page 107 or visit alphausa.org/youthdownloads) *for example timetables that will help you plan.]*

- At the end of the talk, "How Can I Be Filled with the Holy Spirit?" we will have a chance to pray for our groups

- This session is to help train and equip us so we know how to pray for each other

POINT 2 – WHAT IS PRAYER MINISTRY?

- Prayer ministry is where we pray for each other by the laying on of hands

- Jesus prayed for people by placing His hands on them (Luke 4:40)

- The early church prayed for people by placing their hands on them (Acts 8:18)

- Paul tells us to do the same (2 Timothy 1:6)

- People can sometimes be scared about prayer ministry, because they have a false view of who the Holy Spirit is

THE SIMPSONS

PREPARATION TIME **5**
minutes

Quick summary
In this Simpson's clip, we see the faith healer come to town. He is showy and does a rap, while Bart "heals" Homer of having a bucket on his head! This is an example of how the Holy Spirit can be incorrectly portrayed.

Equipment/resources needed
A copy of The Simpsons: *"Faith Off" (season 11, episode 11), Twentieth Century Fox Film Corporation, 2000. Unrated.*

▷ *Chapter 4: 0:08:48*   ☐ *Chapter 4: 0:09:34*

Projector and screen (or a TV), and a DVD player.

How to link to talk
- People can have a false view of the Holy Spirit and prayer ministry because of how it is sometimes portrayed

- We don't need to be worried though, our model of ministry is designed to make it as simple and clear as possible, with no hype

- Prayer ministry is about cooperating with God in what He is doing

- It is always encouraging to read the story of Moses parting the dead sea (Exodus 14)

- When we look at the story, we read that all Moses had to do was stretch out his staff

- It was God who parted the sea! God does the hard bit—we have the easy part

POINT 3 – FOUR VALUES OF PRAYER MINISTRY

1. WE VALUE THE CROSS OF CHRIST

- We want to value the death of Jesus Christ on the cross, because that is central to everything

- Everything we receive is because of the cross, not because of us

- At the foot of the cross we are all the same size

WE'RE ALL THE SAME

PREPARATION TIME **0** minutes

Quick summary
Use this analogy to demonstrate to your team that we are all the same at the foot of the cross.

Equipment / resources needed
None

How it works
- If I compare myself with someone like *[insert the name of one of your friends]* I may think, "Hey, I'm not doing too badly! Compared to him/her, I am a pretty good person." Compared to *[insert name]* I can feel pretty good about myself

- But, if *[insert name]* and I are both at the foot of the cross looking up, we're exactly the same

How to link to talk
- That helps us realize that it's not about you or me, and it's not about some "anointed" person who comes to town—it's about *the* anointed person: Jesus

- It's His anointing, His gifts, His power; it all comes from Him and it's all because of the cross

- If we value the cross of Jesus Christ, we realize that the ultimate and best healing is forgiveness—coming into relationship with Him: that's the root of everything else

- When we value the cross of Jesus we don't pray prayers like this, "Lord, bless and heal Jane because she is such a good person and she really deserves it." Instead we will pray, "Lord, bless and heal Jane because you are such a wonderful God, because you've already done it and you've already earned it"

- We value the cross of Christ and that puts everything else in its place

2. WE VALUE THE BIBLE AS THE WORD OF GOD

- The Bible is our final authority in all matters of faith and conduct

- That doesn't mean that there aren't other authorities, but these all fall under the final authority, which is God's Word

- That means the way we pray needs to come under the scrutiny of Scripture and must conform to what the Bible says

- We sometimes hear bizarre stories about what God is doing. If we value the Bible as God's word, we take those stories we hear, and we check them with the Bible

- There's certainly enough bizarre stuff *in* the Bible to keep us going for ages before we need to start looking for bizarre stuff *outside* it! Like Jesus spitting on mud and rubbing the paste in a man's eyes to heal him—what's that about?

SMITH WIGGLESWORTH

PREPARATION TIME **0** minutes

Quick summary
This true story shows how God used Smith Wigglesworth to perform incredible miracles, but that we look to Jesus, not other people, as our model.

Equipment / resources needed
None

How it works
There was a guy called Smith Wigglesworth, he was born in 1859 and he was a plumber from Bradford, England. He couldn't read or write, but when he became a Christian, his wife taught him how to read as they studied the Bible. He had a simple but profound faith, and he took God at His word. Let me tell you two short stories about what he did.
He once got called to pray for someone, but they died before he got to them. Smith decided that he wasn't going to let death stop him. He went to the morgue, picked up the corpse, held it against the wall and said, "In Jesus' name, I speak life to you and I rebuke death." Then he let go, and the corpse fell to the ground. Now, if that had been me, I'd have looked at the corpse and said, "Well, I had a go, it didn't work—never mind, let's move on." But not our friend Smith. He picked up the corpse, put it against the wall and prayed again, "I speak life to you in Jesus' name." He let go again, and once more, the corpse fell down. He did this a third time, and on the third attempt, the corpse started walking around! Amazing!
On another occasion, Smith Wigglesworth met someone with stomach cancer. As he prayed for them, he punched them really hard in the stomach, and the cancer was healed! (I bet there are some people you'd like to pray for using that method!)

How to link to talk
- Now, we could think "that's a good model for ministry." God used Smith Wigglesworth in some remarkable ways, but Smith is not our model for ministry

- Jesus Christ, as revealed in the Bible, is our model for ministry, so we've got to be people of the book; people who read and study the Bible

3. WE VALUE THE PERSON AND WORK OF THE HOLY SPIRIT

- What does that mean?

- It means it is His work and not ours

- Actually, that is amazing news—we are released from the burden of feeling we have to do something. It is God that does it, not us

WAITERS IN A RESTAURANT

PREPARATION TIME **0** minutes

Quick summary
This analogy which likens us to waiters/waitresses and God to a chef, shows how he is responsible for all the actual work, but how we can help.

Equipment / resources needed
None

How it works
- When we're praying for people we need to look at ourselves like waiters and waitresses in a restaurant
- The customer comes in and we ask them, "What is your order?" and they may say, "A bad left knee, healed please." We write down, "Bad left knee healed" and then we take the order to the chef

How to link to talk
- Only the chef can create the order
- In the same way, only God does the healing and the ministry
- The great thing is that we get to pray—we get to be waiters and waitresses!

JESUS RAISES LAZARUS

PREPARATION TIME **0** minutes

Quick summary
This story shows how prayer is a team effort – we pray, God heals!

Equipment / resources needed
None

How it works
- I love the story in the Bible when Jesus raises Lazarus from the dead (John 11:38-44)
- It was a "team effort"—Jesus and the disciples worked together! In fact, the disciples did two thirds of the work and Jesus only did a third
- Who rolled the stone away? The disciples
- Who took the grave clothes off? The disciples
- The only bit that Jesus did was say, "Lazarus come forth!"

How to link to talk
- We get to be involved—we get to pray—but Jesus does the healing!
- That is great news—it takes away all the burden and stress
- If it's God's work and not ours, we don't need to worry—He will take care of everything. Just keep it simple

4. WE VALUE THE DIGNITY OF THE INDIVIDUAL

- This is really important. We must treat people with respect and dignity, just as we would like to be treated

- If we are praying for someone, the worst thing we can do is get distracted and stop concentrating, that is not affirming and valuing an individual

- The ultimate goal is that the people we pray for meet with Jesus. Sometimes when we pray, it will all seem very gentle. At other times, it might be less gentle—people may laugh or cry, shake, or fall over. All of this is okay, we respect their dignity. We don't need to draw attention to it or make it into a spectacle

- When you have finished praying, you can ask them what happened

- If they say, "Actually, I don't think anything happened," don't be negative. We should simply encourage people that God's Spirit always comes when we ask Him, but we don't always sense what He is doing

- We always say that guys pray with guys and girls pray with girls. This is about respecting people's dignity and making it easier for them to be honest. We all know there will be some things guys won't want to talk about in front of girls and vice versa

POINT 4 – PRACTICAL TIPS

- So, on the weekend, when the speaker ends their talk and invites us to pray to be filled with the Spirit, we will wait on Him for a bit

- The speaker/leader will tell you when to start praying

- No one will be asked to respond, so it's up to you, as leaders and helpers, to offer to pray for each person in your group. It helps if you are already sitting with your group during that session

- You can pray on your own for someone, or in pairs, but no more than two of you should pray for one person at a time, or it can seem a bit intense

- Remember, guys pray with guys, girls pray with girls

- Ask the person if you can pray for them—if they say no, then that's cool, just move on

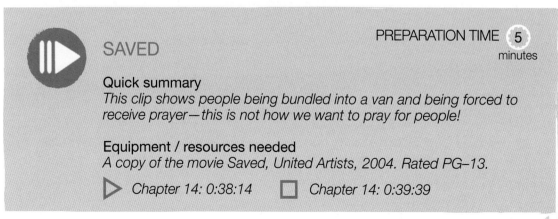

SAVED

PREPARATION TIME ⑤
minutes

Quick summary
This clip shows people being bundled into a van and being forced to receive prayer—this is not how we want to pray for people!

Equipment / resources needed
A copy of the movie Saved, United Artists, 2004. Rated PG–13.

▷ *Chapter 14: 0:38:14*   ☐ *Chapter 14: 0:39:39*

Projector and screen (or a TV), and a DVD player.

How to link to talk
- This is how not to pray, obviously! We never pressure anyone into receiving prayer

The best way to pray for someone who wants it is to:

- Ask permission to place your hand on an appropriate part of their body—their shoulder is probably fine

- **Invite** the Holy Spirit to come. Pray simply, "Come Holy Spirit"

- Then **wait.** This is actually harder than you might think

- Resist the temptation to cover up silence with words. We just need to wait for God to do it

- Then we **watch**. We encourage you to pray with your eyes open. This can seem unnatural, but Jesus told the disciples to "watch and pray" (Matthew 26:41). Jesus said, "I only do what I see my Father doing, I only speak the words my Father gives me to speak"

- Keep your eyes open and watch for what God might be doing

LADY WITH WIG

PREPARATION TIME **0** minutes

Quick summary
This story demonstrates why it's important to pray with your eyes open!

Equipment / resources needed
None.

How it works
This is a story that Mike Pilavachi (Founder and Director of Soul Survivor) tells, which may or may not be true—we really hope it is true!
A lady came up for prayer at a church meeting and a guy started praying for her (remember, *we* would always encourage guys to pray with guys and girls with girls).
He held her head in his hands, closed his eyes and started praying. After a while, he thought she seemed a lot lighter, so he opened his eyes. To his horror, she'd fallen down under the power of the Holy Spirit and he was left holding her wig in his hands while she was lying bald on the floor!
In his panic, he quickly stuffed the wig back on her head before she opened her eyes. When she did open her eyes she started screaming because she thought she'd gone blind—in his haste, he had put the wig on the wrong way round!

How to link to talk
- So we want to pray with our eyes open and watch what God is doing!

- As you pray, if you sense that God is saying something to that person, and it is strengthening, encouraging, and comforting (1 Corinthians 14:3), you can share that

- When you sense they have finished, or that God has done what He wanted to do for now, you can ask them what they sensed/felt

- Then go and pray for someone else!

CONCLUSION

- In a minute we're going to practice praying for each other so that we are all equipped when the weekend comes around

- To summarize, prayer ministry is about cooperating with God

- We need to remember that we value the cross of Christ—so we are ministering to someone on our own level, not someone lesser or better than ourselves

- We need to value the Bible as God's Word

- We need to value the work of the Holy Spirit—it is the Spirit who does the work, not us

- We must value the dignity of each person—we want to bless them and build them up in Christ

- So let's pray for each other!

You may close this part in prayer and ask God to minister to you all by His Spirit.

GROUP ACTIVITY

PRAYER MINISTRY TIME

Ask people of the same sex to get into groups of three (you can do pairs if you prefer). Tell the group that they should each take turns praying for each other—one person "receives" while the other two pray and wait, and then they should swap.

As the leader, you should coach them—while they pray for someone, remind them to:

- Ask permission to place a hand on the person's shoulder

- Ask God's Spirit to come and meet with that person

- Keep your eyes open (you may need to move around to check this —it is usually the most common mistake to make, we naturally close our eyes)

- Remember to wait on God, don't worry about silence

- Watch what God is doing and be open to Him

- When you think you've finished, ask the person what they sensed/felt

- Now swap places

Bring all the groups back together, and ask for some feedback. Ask them:

- How did it go for you?

- What was difficult about it?

- What was easy?

- Do you feel you could do it with your group on the Youth Alpha Weekend/Day?

Ask anyone who has any questions or concerns to meet you at the end.

CLOSE OF SESSION

You might like to close in prayer, praying for the team and the Weekend/Day.

This training session is based on the article "How to pray for each other on Youth Alpha" by Mike Pilavachi. To read the article in full please see page 47.

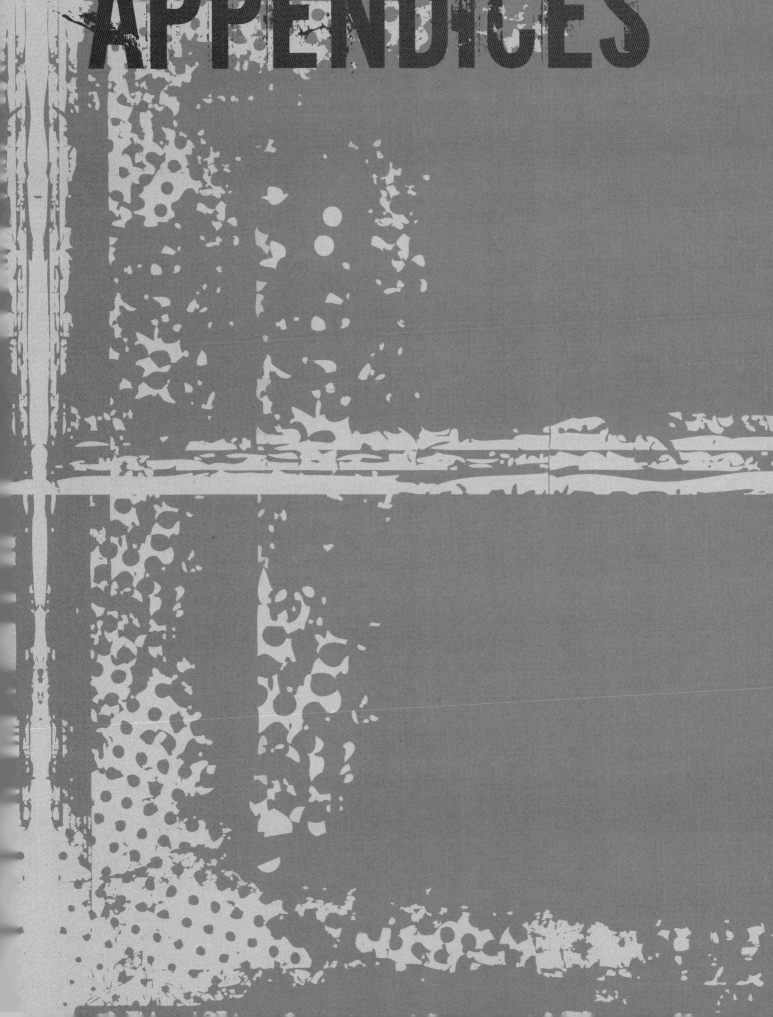

APPENDICES

APPENDIX 1

SAMPLE YOUTH ALPHA COURSE SCHEDULE

The following times are samples to show you how your course could run in either ninety minutes, two hours, or in a thirty minute school lunch break.

A typical afternoon session could look like this:

3:45 P.M.	*Team arrive, set up venue, and pray*
4:30 P.M.	People arrive, food/drinks/snacks served, time to chat
4:55 P.M.	Introduction to session from leader
5:00 P.M.	Ice breaker game
5:10 P.M.	Talk/teaching material presentation
5:30 P.M.	Small group discussion time
6:00 P.M.	Session ends

A typical evening session could look like this:

6:30 P.M.	*Team arrive, set up venue, and pray*
7:00 P.M.	People arrive, food/drinks/snacks served, time to chat
7:30 P.M.	Introduction to session from leader
7:40 P.M.	Ice breaker game
7:50 P.M.	Talk/teaching material presentation
8:10 P.M.	Small group discussion time
8:45 P.M.	Chill-out time
9:00 P.M.	Session ends

A typical school lunchtime session could look like this:

12:30 P.M.	People arrive, eat together, relax, and chat
12:35 P.M.	Talk/teaching material presentation
12:45 P.M.	Small group discussion time
12:55 P.M.	Chill-out time
1:00 P.M.	Session ends

APPENDIX 2

YOUTH ALPHA COURSE – SAMPLE PARENT INFORMATION SHEET

This is a sample hand out only. You can find an amendable template online at alphausa.org/youthdownloads which can be adapted to fit the context of your course.

[INSERT NAME OF CHURCH, E.G.: ST. STEPHEN'S CHURCH] YOUTH ALPHA COURSE – PARENT INFORMATION SHEET

WHAT IS YOUTH ALPHA?

Youth Alpha is a fun, informative, and relaxed course that offers teenagers the chance to explore some of the bigger questions of life, while teaching the basics of the Christian faith.

Youth Alpha is based on the Alpha course, which is now running in over 160 countries worldwide. Over 15 million people have attended a course, and it is running in every major Christian denomination around the world.

For more information please visit alphausa.org/youth

WHAT HAPPENS AT YOUTH ALPHA?

Each session of Youth Alpha has four main elements—food, fun, a short presentation, and discussion in small groups.

At each session, one of the team will give a short presentation on a different aspect of the Christian faith (covering topics such as "Who Is Jesus?," "Why and How Do I Pray?," and "What about the Church?" among others).

Following the presentation, there will be discussion time in small groups. Here, the groups are encouraged to be completely honest, say exactly how they feel about what has been said and debate the topics together. All opinions are considered valid, and there is no pressure to think or act in a particular way.

It is worth mentioning that no session is compulsory, and guests are welcome to leave the course at any point. The course provides an opportunity for anyone, regardless of background, to make an informed choice for themselves.

WHO IS RUNNING IT?

This Youth Alpha course is being run by [insert name(s)] and a team from [insert church or youth center name (if applicable)].

WHAT ARE THE PRACTICAL DETAILS?

Youth Alpha will run weekly on [insert day and time of day, e.g.: Wednesday evenings] from [insert start time, e.g.: 7 P.M.] to [insert end time, e.g.: 9 P.M.] at [insert venue details].

There is an optional weekend/day [delete as appropriate] in the middle of the course which we would love your teenager to come to. We are currently finalizing arrangements for this, and more information will be provided near the start of the course.

DOES IT COST MONEY?

The course itself is totally free—food will be provided for an optional donation of [insert suggested donation, e.g.: $3]. There will also be a suggested cost for the weekend/day [delete as appropriate] which we will confirm soon, but we would hate anyone to miss out due to financial reasons so please let us know if this may be a problem.

WHO CAN I CONTACT FOR MORE INFORMATION?

Please contact [insert name] on [insert phone number] or by email on [insert email address].

If you are interested in the topics covered on Youth Alpha and would like to find out more about attending an Alpha course yourself, please just ask one of the team or visit alpha.org to find a local course.

We hope this answers your questions. If not, please feel free to contact us; we would love to speak to you.

APPENDIX 3

SAMPLE YOUTH ALPHA WEEKEND/DAY PROGRAM

FRIDAY

7:00 P.M.	Arrive
8:00 P.M.	Evening meal
9:00 P.M.	Short introductory session*, including:
	• Ice breaker games
	• Short time of worship
	• Brief overview of weekend, prayer
Late activity	Bonfire, late night hike, big-screen movie, etc.

SATURDAY

9:00 A.M.	Breakfast
10:00 A.M.	Weekend Session 1, including:
	• Ice breaker games
	• Worship
	• Talk—"What about the Holy Spirit?"
11:30 A.M.	Break
12:00 P.M.	Small groups
1:00 P.M.	Lunch
2:00 P.M.	Afternoon activities, sports, or visit to an attraction
4:15 P.M.	Afternoon snack (for those who are starving)
5:00 P.M.	Weekend Session 2, including:
	• Ice breaker games
	• Worship
	• Talk—"How Can I Be Filled with the Holy Spirit?"
	• Prayer ministry
7 P.M.	Evening meal
8 P.M.	Entertainment: movie, talent show, etc.

*The suggested weekend introductory session is entirely optional, and no teaching material has been produced for this. We would suggest you simply welcome people to the weekend, run through the program for the weekend, and introduce the theme of the person and work of the Holy Spirit. It should not be a full talk—just opening remarks.

APPENDIX 3 (continued)

SUNDAY

9:00 A.M.	Breakfast
10:00 A.M.	Small groups
11:00 A.M.	Weekend Session 3, including:

- Ice breaker games
- Worship
- Talk – "How Can I Make the Most of the Rest of My Life?"
- Prayer ministry

1:00 P.M.	Lunch
2:00 P.M.	Travel home

SAMPLE YOUTH ALPHA DAY PROGRAM

9:30 A.M.	Arrival and breakfast
10:00 A.M.	Weekend Session 1, including:

- Ice breaker games
- Worship
- Talk – "What about the Holy Spirit?"

11:30 A.M.	Break
11:45 A.M.	Small groups
12:30 P.M.	Lunch
1:30 P.M.	Afternoon activities, sports, or visit to an attraction
3:30 P.M.	Weekend Session 2, including:

- Ice breaker games
- Worship
- Talk – "How Can I Be Filled with the Holy Spirit?"
- Prayer ministry

5:00 P.M.	Drinks and snacks
5:30 P.M.	End of day

APPENDIX 4

YOUTH ALPHA WEEKEND/DAY – SAMPLE PARENT INFORMATION SHEET/BOOKING FORM

This is a sample hand out only. You can find an amendable template online at www.alphausa.org/youthdownloads which can be adapted to fit the context of your course.

[INSERT NAME OF CHURCH, E.G.: ST. STEPHEN'S CHURCH] YOUTH ALPHA WEEKEND/DAY [DELETE AS APPLICABLE] – PARENT INFORMATION SHEET

WHAT HAPPENS AT THE YOUTH ALPHA WEEKEND/DAY? [DELETE AS APPLICABLE]

The Youth Alpha Weekend/Day [delete as applicable] offers teenagers a chance to continue their Youth Alpha journey with a bit more time to hang out together. The Weekend/Day [delete as applicable] will be packed full of fun activities, as well the usual Youth Alpha sessions, including more presentations and small group discussions.

The Weekend/Day [delete as applicable] will focus on the work of the Holy Spirit in the lives of Christians. There will also be an opportunity for the group to pray together. As always, we can assure you that there will be no pressure on anyone to pray, sing, or participate in anything that they do not wish to. The weekend is entirely voluntary, and it is up to you whether your teenager comes.

Activities such as [insert activities you intend to do here] will form a major part of the Weekend/Day [delete as applicable] and all meals will be provided from [Friday dinner] through to [Sunday lunch].

WHO IS RUNNING IT?

This Youth Alpha course is being run by [insert name(s)] and a team from [insert church or youth center name (if applicable)].

All adult helpers have had a background check and we will have someone qualified in first aid with us.

DOES IT COST MONEY?

Obviously, it does cost money for us to run the Weekend/Day [delete as applicable]. We are suggesting that people pay a fee of $__ [insert decided fee] to attend (includes all meals, accommodation, and activities), but scholarships are available for anyone who cannot pay the full amount. Please speak to one of the team for information regarding scholarships [if applicable to your course]. The fee is payable in [insert methods of payment accepted, e.g.: cash, check (remember to include details on who to make the check payable to), etc.].

WHAT ARE THE PRACTICAL DETAILS?

We will be holding the Weekend/Day [delete as applicable] at [venue name and address details]. We will be travelling there by [insert mode of transportation] together. We will meet on [insert date, e.g.: Friday September 24] at [insert time, e.g.: 6 P.M.] to leave at [insert time, e.g.: 6:15 P.M.] and plan to return at [insert time, e.g.: 9 P.M.] on [insert date, e.g.: Sunday September 26].

WHO CAN I CONTACT FOR MORE INFORMATION?

Please contact [insert name] on [insert phone number] or by email on [insert email address].

The emergency contact for the venue is [insert number].

HOW CAN WE REGISTER?

Each person attending needs to fill in a registration form which must be signed by a parent or guardian. Relevant medical and dietary information must be included. Please return the form and payment to one of the Youth Alpha team as soon as possible in order to guarantee a place.

We hope this answers your questions. If not, please feel free to contact us; we would love to speak to you.

[INSERT NAME OF CHURCH, E.G.: ST. STEPHEN'S CHURCH] YOUTH ALPHA WEEKEND/DAY [DELETE AS APPLICABLE] – BOOKING FORM

GUESTS' PART

Name:
Address:
Email:
Cell number:
Date of birth:

I would love to come to the Youth Alpha Weekend/Day [delete as applicable] at [insert name of venue]. I agree to abide by all the rules of the Weekend/Day under the leadership of the Youth Alpha team.

Signed: _____   Date: _____

PARENTS' PART

Parent/guardian name(s):
Address (if different from above):
Email(s):
Home telephone number(s):
Cell number(s):
Other emergency contact (24 hrs):
Medical requirements:
Dietary needs:
Allergies:
Doctor's name:
Doctor's phone number:

☐ I agree to _____ attending the Youth Alpha Weekend at [insert name of venue] from [insert start date, e.g.: September 24] – [insert end date, e.g.: September 26] [insert year, e.g.: 2010] and entrust them to the leaders' responsible care while they are participating in the Youth Alpha Weekend/Day [delete as applicable] Away program. I understand that they will be travelling by [insert mode of transportation].

☐ I give my permission for the leaders or venue staff to treat my child for minor medical needs, including administration of pain medication (such as Tylenol and Ibuprofen) as needed.

☐ I enclose cash/a check for the sum of [$ insert decided fee] (payable to "[insert name to whom the check is payable]").

☐ I have described any relevant medical, dietary, and allergy details above. In case of an emergency, I can be contacted at the number(s) above.

Signed: _____ (parent/guardian)   Date: _____

PLEASE RETURN THIS SLIP TO [INSERT LEADERS' NAME] **WITH THE CORRECT PAYMENT AS SOON AS POSSIBLE TO ENSURE A PLACE.**